Effective Communication in Multicultural Health Care Settings

Communicating Effectively in Multicultural Contexts

Series Editors: William B. Gudykunst and Stella Ting-Toomey

Department of Speech Communication
California State University, Fullerton

The books in this series are designed to help readers communicate effectively in various multicultural contexts. Authors of the volumes in the series translate relevant communication theories to provide readable and comprehensive descriptions of the various multicultural contexts. Each volume contains specific suggestions for how readers can communicate effectively with members of different cultures and/ or ethnic groups in the specific contexts covered in the volume. The volumes should appeal to people interested in developing multicultural awareness or improving their communication skills, as well as anyone who works in a multicultural setting.

Volumes in this series

1. **BRIDGING JAPANESE/NORTH AMERICAN DIFFERENCES**
   William B. Gudykunst and Tsukasa Nishida

2. **INTERCULTURAL COMMUNICATION TRAINING:**
   An Introduction
   Richard W. Brislin and Tomoko Yoshida

3. **EFFECTIVE COMMUNICATION IN MULTICULTURAL**
   HEALTH CARE SETTINGS
   Gary L. Kreps and Elizabeth N. Kunimoto

EFFECTIVE COMMUNICATION IN MULTICULTURAL HEALTH CARE SETTINGS

GARY L. KREPS
ELIZABETH N. KUNIMOTO

SAGE Publications
International Educational and Professional Publisher
Thousand Oaks   London   New Delhi

For information address:

 SAGE Publications, Inc.
2455 Teller Road
Thousand Oaks, California 91320

SAGE Publications Ltd.
6 Bonhill Street
London EC2A 4PU
United Kingdom

SAGE Publications India Pvt. Ltd.
M-32 Market
Greater Kailash I
New Delhi 110 048 India

Printed in the United States of America

Library of Congress Cataloging-in-Publication Data

Kreps, Gary L.
   Effective communication in multicultural health care settings/
Gary L. Kreps, Elizabeth N. Kunimoto.
      p. cm. — (Communicating effectively in multicultural
contexts ; 3)
   Includes bibliographical references and index.
   ISBN 0-8039-4713-5. — ISBN 0-8039-4714-3 (pbk.)
   1. Communication in medicine. 2. Intercultural communication.
3. Medical personnel and patient. 4. Interpersonal communication.
I. Kunimoto, Elizabeth N. II. Title. III. Series
R118.K729   1994
610.69'6—dc20   94-2011

      95 96 97 98 10 9 8 7 6 5 4 3 2

Sage Production Editor: Astrid Virding

Contents

Preface

This book is designed to provide insights into the complexities of multicultural relations in health care, to demystify the many cultural influences on health and health care, and to help individuals who participate in the modern health care system (whether as health care providers, administrators, staff members, consumers, or as friends and family members of health care consumers) become effective multicultural communicators. Each chapter is begun with a haiku written specifically for this book by Liz Kunimoto. We humbly hope that this book helps its readers begin a process of self-examination, social analysis, and competency building that will enable them to interact sensitively and strategically in effectively negotiating their way beyond the bureaucracy and complexities of the modern health care system to accomplish their personal and professional goals. Ultimately, we hope this book helps people get the most benefit they can out of health care and facilitates the promotion of public health.

There are many people who helped us think through the ideas presented here and supported us in the writing of this book. We owe a real debt of gratitude to Stella Ting-Toomey and Bill Gudykunst, who graciously invited us to write this book as part of their Communicating Effectively in Multicultural Contexts Series. Our thanks also to the Sage Publications editorial staff for their patient and professional help in the production of this book. We appreciate the support and stimulating ideas of our colleagues at Northern Illinois University, the University of Hawaii at Manoa, and the Health Communication Interest Groups of both the International Communication Association and the Speech Communication Association. Our thanks to the BITNET and INTERNET systems for facilitating frequent electronic communication between Illinois and Hawaii. Most of all, however, we sincerely thank our families for supporting us through the many late hours, frustrations, and distractions we experienced in writing this book. We hope that our efforts and the support of so many have resulted in a book that will help others improve the quality of their lives, enjoy their interactions with others, and promote a spirit of *ohana* (togetherness)!

Gary L. Kreps
St. Charles, Illinois

Elizabeth N. Kunimoto
Honolulu, Hawaii

Overview of Multicultural Communication in Health Care

Culture, the milieu
Of attitudes and values,
Affects all choices.

◆ The Nature of Culture

Culture is a complex and multifaceted social phenomenon that has powerful influences on all aspects of modern life. Culture refers to the collective sensemaking of members of social groups, the shared ways they make sense of reality. Culture consists of shared beliefs, values, and attitudes that guide the behaviors of group members (Geertz, 1973; Gudykunst, Ting-Toomey, & Chua, 1988; Kreps, 1990a). Brown explains that culture "refers to all the accepted and patterned ways of behavior of a given people. It is a body of common understandings. It is the sum total and the organization or arrangement of all the group's ways of thinking, feeling, and acting" (1963, pp. 3-4).

The term *culture* is often used to describe very large social groupings of people based on shared national origin. For example, the terms *American culture, Chinese culture,* or *Nigerian culture* describe people who are indigenous to each of these countries. National cultures have enormous influences on behavior, but cultural membership operates at a wide range of levels and is certainly not limited to just nationalities. Culture refers to a wide range of different social groups that influence members' beliefs, attitudes, and behaviors. Kreps and Thornton (1984) explain, "Within the United States, for example, women have a somewhat separate culture from men, blacks from Indians, and children from the elderly. In the area of health care, physicians have a culture different from that of other health care providers. Language, friendship, eating habits, communication practices, music, social acts, economic and political activities, and technology dictate culture and its different groupings" (p. 192). Culture also includes a broad range of social factors that lead people to think and act in very unique ways. In this book we will look at many different cultural groups and examine a wide range of cultural influences on people participating in the health care system.

Within nations, there are regional cultures that influence member behaviors. For example, within the United States it is common to hear people talk about Midwesterners or Southerners or New Englanders as regional cultural groups. There are also cultural groups that are rooted in ethnic, racial, and religious commonalities, such as the Mexican-American culture, the Jewish culture, the Moslem culture, the African-American culture, or the WASP (White Anglo-Saxon Protestant) culture. Biological gender (whether you are a male or a female) exerts a powerful cultural influence on behavior, with men and women displaying distinct socially learned beliefs, attitudes, and values. (The "double-standard" that describes different social rules and expectations for men and women is a clear illustration of the cultural influence of gender). People of different ages, educational levels, socioeconomic standing, occupations, sexual orientations, and even of different health conditions belong to their own cultural groups. Even persons who share certain health conditions, such as people who are blind, deaf, or paralyzed, have their own cultural orientations, as do people who are dying, or who have diabetes, cancer, or AIDS. In this book, we will attempt to examine the influences of these many different cultural orientations on communication in the provision of health care.

Every individual is composed of a unique combination of different cultural orientations and influences, and every person belongs to many different cultural groups. It is important that we recognize the influences of many cultures on our lives. Based on our heritage and life experiences we each develop our own idiosyncratic multicultural identity. For example, the authors of this book each have unique cultural identities. By sharing with you an abbreviated list of several major cultural influences on each of our lives we hope to dramatically illustrate the multicultural nature of individual identities and help you get to know us a little better. Gary Kreps is a large (read overweight), American Caucasian male, Ph.D., college professor, social scientist, author, researcher, organizational consultant, editor, public speaker, gerontologist, humanist, feminist, asthmatic, flower child of the sixties and seventies, nature lover, and film buff, who has worked in many different blue-collar and white-collar jobs, is of Eastern European ancestry, was raised in the Jewish faith, is an overachiever (read workaholic), likes to laugh and make others laugh, is impatient, is aggressive—but learning to become more interpersonally sensitive, is a native New Yorker, was educated on the West Coast, has lived most of his adult years in the Midwest, is a doting father of two young children, and is a loving husband. Liz Kunimoto is a petite (read short), Asian-American female, Ph.D., professor, and educational psychologist, whose parents emigrated from Hiroshima, who was born in Hawaii and educated in Ann Arbor, Michigan, is the wife of a tamed samurai, is a formerly submissive Japanese housewife who is rapidly learning to become assertive, is a mother of three articulate professionals, was an advocate for her 83-year-old mother and 96-year-old father-in-law until their deaths recently, and is a poet, artist, researcher in health communication, and citizen of the world, an identity that was born out of multicultural interaction with international students at Ann Arbor. Whew, how's that for self-disclosure?

We each are the products of multiple cultural memberships. We are multicultural individuals. Whenever people communicate there are multiple cultural influences on their interaction. That is why we chose to use the term *multicultural* in this book to describe human communication, as opposed to using the term *intercultural*, which suggests a more limited recognition of the number of cultural perspectives involved in communication. Even when we communicate with ourselves, *intrapersonally*, our communication is influenced by our multiple cultural affiliations. In making everyday decisions, such as what clothes to wear, what food to eat, or how to greet another person, we are choosing from a wide range of culturally acquired social guidelines to direct our behavior. Since every person has a unique combination of cultural influences, the cultural guidelines and the behavioral choices made by individuals are very idiosyncratic. The term *multicultural* recognizes the complex influences of multiple cultural orientations on behavior and illustrates the multicultural nature of human communication.

Take a moment to compose a list of cultural descriptors that describe who you are. Be sure to consider including such relevant cultural influences as your gender, age, race, religion, national origin, health status, socioeconomic status, education level, and occupation. Each of the current cultural descriptors you have identified influences who you are, how you perceive the world, and how you behave. It is important to recognize that over time your cultural descriptors will change. You will gain new cultural influences and former cultural descriptors will become less influential in your life. To communicate effectively with others it is important to understand and respect the different cultural orientations that currently influence the ways each person thinks and acts. In this book, we describe strategies for increasing intercultural sensitivity and understanding, which are prerequisites to effective multicultural communication.

◆ Multicultural Influences on Modern Health Care

The modern health care system is a cultural melting pot, comprised of individuals from different combinations of national, regional, ethnic, racial, socioeconomic, occupational, generational, and health-status cultural orientations. For example, it is becoming increasingly common to encounter foreign-born and foreign-educated health care providers working in American hospitals, and as the American population becomes more multicultural there are increasing numbers of foreign-born individuals seeking health care. It is easy to recognize how any two people from different nationalities might have difficulties communicating in health care situations, at the least because they are likely to speak different languages, which may limit their ability to understand each other. Even if they speak English as a second language, they may not have complete mastery of this second language, which limits the effectiveness of their communication. Furthermore, they are likely to have conflicting assumptions and expectations about health and health care due to their culturally based *health beliefs*.

The example of how different nationalities can act as cultural barriers to effective health communication is just the tip of the iceberg; there are many other, sometimes not as obvious, cultural barriers to effective communication in the modern health care system that lie beneath the water's surface. The "iceberg" model of multicultural influences on communication (see Figure 1.1) illustrates that while some of an individual's cultural influences may be readily apparent, others are hidden and may not be immediately recognized in initial interactions. Yet these hidden cultural factors can have major influences on communication in health care contexts. The multicultural influences on modern health care are not just limited to differences in nationality. The sex, age, educational background, or occupation of health care consumers and providers may also act as cultural barriers to effective health communication. In this book, we will examine the influences of these many cultural differences on the provision of effective and satisfying health care

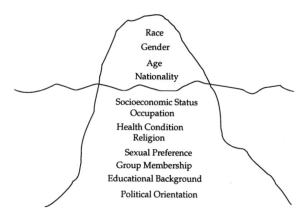

Figure 1.1. Iceberg Model of Multicultural Influences on Communication

and describe how these potential cultural barriers, if approached strategically, can actually be used to facilitate effective health communication.

Health care consumers and providers approach health care situations with their own unique communication characteristics, health beliefs, and customs, based on their personal backgrounds, that dramatically influence their health care needs and the health behaviors they choose to engage in (see, e.g., Waxler-Morrison, Anderson, & Richardson, 1990). Developing effective multicultural relations between culturally unique participants in the modern health care system is a prerequisite to effective health care delivery (Howe-Murphy, Ross, Tseng, & Hartwig, 1989; McNeil, 1990). Participants in the health care system are interdependent. They must share relevant information and coordinate many different activities to effectively accomplish their health care goals (Kreps, 1988b; Kreps & Thornton, 1992). Health care providers depend on receiving accurate information from their clients about health histories and symptoms to make informed diagnoses. Similarly, consumers depend on receiving clear and descriptive information about proposed health care treatment strategies from their doctors (or other health care providers) so these consumers can provide informed consent to pursue the prescribed health care procedures (Alfidi, 1971).

Members of health care teams (i.e., physicians from different areas of specialization, nurses, therapists, social workers, and clients) also depend on sharing pertinent treatment information with one another to provide effective care. Yet, the members of these health care teams are likely to have very different, and often conflicting, orientations to providing health care, based on their professional training as well as other multicultural differences. For example, within a typical health care team, each member has his or her own agenda for treatment. The surgeon is likely to focus on planning surgical procedures, the psychiatrist may be concerned with psychiatric evaluation and intervention, the nurse may be concerned with promoting client comfort and patient management, the physical therapist may be concerned with long-term rehabilitation strategies, the social worker may be concerned with helping the client adapt to his or her social environment, while the client is likely to be most concerned with receiving effective, timely, painless, and inexpensive treatment. These different points of focus provide health care teams with both advantages and disadvantages. Multiple points of view help team members generate a broad base of information about health care treatment that encourages a *holistic* (full) view of the client's condition, needs, and health care treatment. The different cultural perspectives also can complicate health care, however, especially if there is a lack of respect for members' different orientations, leading to unnecessary competition and unprofitable conflict among members of the health care team. Effective multicultural communication can promote the holistic benefits of health care teams, by encouraging interpersonal respect and minimizing unproductive competition between team members.

The sharing of relevant health information provides health care consumers with a rationale and direction for coordination and cooperation in health care practice (Kreps, 1988a; 1988b). Such cooperation is dramatically complicated by abundant evidence of widespread ignorance and insensitivity to cultural differences in health care (Helman, 1990; Kleinman, 1980; Kreps, 1988b; Spector, 1979). Health care providers and consumers depend on their abilities to communicate sensitively and effectively with one another to relieve discomfort, save lives, and promote health (Kreps & Thornton, 1992). Ineffective intercultural communication in health care can and often does result in unnecessary pain, suffering, and death.

◆ Cultural Ethnocentrism in Modern Health Care

The lack of cultural sensitivity evident in health care is certainly not indigenous to only the health care system; it is a widespread malignancy of modern organizational life (Joy, 1987). Yet, ineffective intercultural communication is exacerbated in health care for several reasons. For example, people seeking health care, especially those who are fearful, uncomfortable, and/or in pain, are generally too preoccupied with their own physical condition to pay particular attention to communicating effectively with health care providers and staff. Health care professionals are often so focused on the instrumental activities of providing health care that they have a tendency to neglect to interact personally and caringly with their clients (Kreps & Thornton, 1992; Masi, 1988). Health care participants also often adopt an emergency, high-pressure mind-set, where time is of the essence and they are too rushed to provide the personal attention necessary for sensitive intercultural relations. Interprofessional cultural barriers often encourage a sense of competition between interdependent health care providers and limit the expression of mutual respect and cooperation among these members of the health care team (Burner, Cunningham, & Hattar, 1990; Kreps & Thornton, 1992).

Because the individuals who participate in the modern health care system represent such a broad range of different cultural beliefs, attitudes, and values, modern health care has inevitably become an increasingly multicultural enterprise. In such an environment, effective health care delivery demands sensitivity to cultural differences. The plethora of different cultural orientations represented in modern health care inevitably results in divergent interpretations of health problems and conflicting selection of strategies for addressing these problems. Unfortunately, modern Western health care systems tend to be very ethnocentric and bureaucratic, proselytizing consumers to "comply" with formalized, often technologically based, and scientifically justified forms of treatment. Such treatment strategies are likely to violate many consumers' personally held cultural beliefs about health care and can result in strong resistance to prescribed health care regimens, especially if there is not sensitive intercultural communication between providers and consumers.

Ethnocentrism refers to the tendency of members of a particular cultural group to view their own cultural orientation as the only legitimate perspective on reality. Ethnocentric individuals often evaluate the cultural orientations of people from different orientations and backgrounds as wrong, evil, and dangerous. They have little tolerance and respect for people from "opposing" cultural points of view. People who see the world differently than they do are seen as being misinformed and even dangerous.

Ethnocentrism occurs as a result of cultural socialization processes that are too effective. *Socialization* is a process that is used to teach and reinforce cultural rules to members within a culture. Communication is the primary tool of socialization. Members are given specialized evaluative feedback about their behaviors from other members of the culture to let them know when their actions are in accordance with cultural rules. This specialized form of feedback is known as *metacommunication*, or communication about the way a person communicates that encourages culturally "correct" behavior.

Metacommunication reinforces culturally "correct" behavior by providing positive evaluations (approval and praise) to those who follow the rules (norms). Metacommunication is also used to eliminate culturally "incorrect" behavior by providing negative evaluations (disapproval and condemnation) to the actor who dares to violate cultural norms. Socialization is a very powerful process, because within a given culture members are provided with continuous, unanimous support for following cultural norms for behavior. If a person wants to be accepted and liked by others within a culture he or she had better follow cultural rules. Violating cultural rules is dangerous. Socialization is an important process by which cultural members are indoctrinated in the ways of the culture and assimilated into the culture.

Socialization can go too far, however, when ethnocentric members of Culture A believe they must force members of Culture B to give up their own cultural orientation and adopt the norms of Culture A. This attempt to force others to give up their own cultural norms and adopt another set of norms is known as *proselytizing*. Proselytizing demonstrates a clear lack of respect for the legitimacy of others' cultural background. It asserts that my cultural perspective is superior to yours. Obviously, people do not usually react positively to proselytizing. They are insulted and offended by the lack of respect for their beliefs, attitudes, and values that proselytizing infers. Attempts to force others to give up their personal culturally approved beliefs and behaviors can lead to anger and resentment and is a common reason for ineffective communication in health care.

◆ Valuing Cultural Diversity

In this book we recommend the development and expression of genuine interest and respect for different cultural orientations. Not only should we be tolerant of different cultural perspectives, we should also demonstrate active interest and admiration for the cultural norms of other cultures. We must clearly recognize the great value of cultural diversity. By recognizing that cultural norms do not develop haphazardly—they are developed specifically to help cultural members cope with the many constraints they face in the world—we recognize the information value of learning about other cultures and interacting with members of different cultures.

Cultural exploration can teach us a great deal and help us appreciate the great beauty in the different ways that cultures frame reality, establish social organization, and accomplish different goals. For example, the history, government, art, music, literature, foods, and familial structures of different cultures are intricate, idiosyncratic, and fascinating. The norms governing these different aspects of life develop specifically to help cultural groups accomplish their goals within unique physical, social, and political environments. By examining these cultural norms we learn new ways of interpreting and responding to different environments, increase our sophistication and understanding of the world, enhance our abilities to interact meaningfully with people from different cultures, and learn about the differences and commonalities between different cultures.

The exploration of different cultures can help us learn about new ways of interpreting reality and increase our understanding of other people, their experiences, and the world they live in. The demonstration of respect and interest in the cultural perspectives of others can also serve as a foundation for developing supportive and cooperative relationships with people from different cultures. The *norm of reciprocity* is a general rule of human behavior that asserts that we feel obliged to respond to others in a manner that is complementary to the way they act toward us (Kreps, 1990a). The expression of respect and interest validates the legitimacy and worth of others' cultural backgrounds, encourages their reciprocal interest in our cultural orientation, and provides a basis for communication. Mutual exploration of cultural similarities and differences between members of two different cultures helps make the implicit norms of these different cultures explicit. By learning about each others' rules, expectations, and motivations for behavior, we can diminish the potential of violating each others' cultural norms and encourage the growth of reciprocal respect and cooperation. We also become more multicultural ourselves by learning about and adopting ideas and rituals from other cultures, which increases our abilities to understand different cultural perspectives, adapt to different situations, and interact effectively with representatives of different cultures.

The *theory of weak ties* suggests that the information value (new information) to be gained by communicating with others from very different cultural orientations is much greater than the information value of interacting with people who share similar cultural perspectives (Granovetter, 1973; Kreps, 1990a; Liu & Duff, 1972; Rogers & Agarwal-Rogers, 1976). People from different cultures have more new information to offer each other than people from similar cultures. People who share similar cultural backgrounds are likely to see the world in very similar ways and develop similar solutions to problems. Although this is comforting and reinforcing for us, it does not provide us with innovative ideas and creative solutions to problems. People who share different cultural backgrounds are likely to see the world very differently and develop different solutions to the same problems. These differences can be challenging and uncomfortable for us because they question the legitimacy of our own cultural orientations. However, if we recognize that there are many different legitimate perspectives on and interpretations of reality, as well as many different ways to solve problems, we welcome the new information gained from divergent cultural orientations.

Unfortunately, although interaction with people from different cultural orientations is likely to provide us with rich new information, it is also more difficult to communicate effectively with those who are different from us than it is to communicate with those who are similar to us. We are more likely to understand and less likely to violate cultural norms of those who are similar to us because we probably already understand and conform to the cultural guidelines that govern their behaviors. It is easier for us to understand those who are similar to us because we probably use the same languages and communication rituals and are probably familiar with the ideas and logics culturally similar individuals are likely to espouse. To communicate effectively with those who are culturally dissimilar to us, we must be willing to endure the discomfort of unfamiliarity and uncertainty. We must work to overcome communication barriers, to understand different languages, rituals, logics, and norms. We must be open-minded and receptive. If we can develop the ability to communicate effectively with those who are culturally dissimilar, we can learn a great deal from our interactions.

The systems theory principle of *equifinality* suggests that the attainment of system goals is not determined solely by the initial conditions confronting the system; system goals can be reached from different initial conditions in many different ways (Bertalanffy, 1968; Kreps, 1990a). There are many different ways of accomplishing goals, based on different environmental conditions and constraints. Exploration of different cultural perspectives can increase our abilities to achieve our goals by helping to identify different strategies for solving complex problems, such as health care problems. Modern health care knowledge is by no means complete. There is much more that health care professionals do not know about diagnosing and treating health care problems than there is that they do know. Effective multicultural communication in health care can help provide participants in the health care delivery system with new information and strategies for responding to complex health care problems. The valuing of cultural diversity in health care can help enhance the effectiveness of health care delivery.

◆ A Systemic Orientation to
Multicultural Communication in Health Care

Communication occurs at many different interdependent hierarchical levels of analysis (Kreps, 1988b). In this book, we will examine multicultural communication in health care at the intrapersonal, interpersonal, group, organizational, and societal levels of analysis, as depicted in the Hierarchical Levels of Multicultural Communication Model (see Figure 1.2). Interpersonal communication builds on intrapersonal interaction. Group communication builds on both intrapersonal and interpersonal

Figure 1.2. Hierarchical Levels of Multicultural Communication Model

interactions. Organizational communication builds on the previous three, intrapersonal, interpersonal, and group interactions. Societal communication, the largest level of communication to be addressed in this book, builds on intrapersonal, interpersonal, group, and organizational interactions.

The most basic level of human communication is *intrapersonal communication*, where we interact with ourselves in interpreting reality and creating messages for communicating with others. The central communicative processes of encoding and decoding are performed at the intrapersonal level of communication. Encoding and decoding are translation processes that help us coordinate our use of *meanings* and *messages*, the two basic building blocks of human communication. *Encoding* is the process by which we translate our own personally held meanings into messages; *decoding* is the process by which we translate the messages we receive into personally held meanings. These processes enable us to link messages and meanings, strategically using our meanings to create messages and making sense out of the messages we encounter. Culture has strong influences on both encoding and decoding processes because culture provides us with guidelines for creating appropriate messages for different situations and audiences and also provides us with logics for interpreting and understanding different messages. In Chapter 2 of this book we examine intrapersonal communication by describing the influences of communication on individual health, especially psychological health.

Interpersonal communication involves interaction between two individuals that enables them to develop and maintain a relationship. Interpersonal communication is often referred to as *relational* or *dyadic* communication to illustrate the mutual adjustment of two partners at this level of interaction. Intrapersonal communication is the foundation on which interpersonal communication is built. To communicate effectively interpersonally, relational partners must each first engage in effective intrapersonal interaction. If interactants are not effectively communicating intrapersonally (creating and interpreting messages), it is unlikely that they will be able to communicate effectively at the interpersonal level. Interpersonal communication is more complex than intrapersonal communication because it involves relational negotiation between two different individuals who are unlikely to see the world in the same way. Relational partners use interpersonal communication to express their different interpretations of reality and negotiate the fulfillment of their individual goals and needs. When interpersonal interactants represent very different cultural perspectives, interpersonal accommodation becomes very challenging because the relational partners are likely to interpret the world very differently and have different goals and needs. In Chapter 3 we examine the interpersonal communication level, describing the centrality of interpersonal relationships in the provision of health care and illustrating many of the challenges of bridging cultural differences in developing and maintaining effective multicultural health care relationships.

Group communication refers to the interaction of three or more individuals to adapt to their environment and achieve commonly recognized goals (Kreps, 1990a). Groups are formed to work together on tasks that might be too difficult for individuals to accomplish alone. Group communication is complex. It involves negotiation among many interpersonal relationships established between different group members. These relationships are often used politically in groups to form coalitions that influence group activities and outcomes. In effective groups, members work together cooperatively. Such groups benefit from *synergy*, the ability to generate greater outputs through cooperative action. Communication should be used to promote cooperation within groups, enabling group members to work together harmoniously and productively. Unfortunately, cooperation does not always occur naturally, and ineffective group communication leads more often to competition than cooperation. Cultural differences among group members can increase the knowledge-base of the group, but if group members are ethnocentric these differences can also increase group tension. In Chapter 4 we describe some of the challenges of effective multicultural group communication in health care and identify several strategies for using cultural diversity to promote group processes and outcomes.

Organizational communication refers to the communication used to promote social organization through the coordination of interdependent groups. This level of communication encompasses intrapersonal, interpersonal, and group communication. Because of both the size of modern organizations and the diversity of activities performed in organizational life, it is important to develop effective formal channels and informal (emergent) networks of communication to connect different horizontal task groups and divisions as well as different hierarchical (vertical) levels within the organization to promote the sharing of relevant information throughout the organization. Shared information is essential to accomplishing organizational goals because relevant information provides organization members with rationale and direction for coordinating their activities (Kreps, 1990a). In Chapter 5 we examine organizational communication by describing the multicultural makeup of modern health care systems and providing strategies for promoting multicultural cooperation in organizations. This chapter also examines some of the interprofessional cultural issues that influence the performance of health care delivery systems.

Societal communication refers to the coordination of different groups and organizations with large social systems. Societal communication involves the coordination of many organizations representing government, industry, and education to fulfill societal goals of peace, prosperity, and health. Societal communication encompasses all of the previous levels of communication (intrapersonal, interpersonal, group, and organizational). Many communication channels and media are used, including mass media, to provide relevant information to the many different individuals, groups, and organizations that comprise modern societies. An important health care function of societal communication is to promote public health and prevent the spread of dangerous health risks. In Chapter 6 we examine the role of communication in promoting public health within societies. The multicultural makeup of modern societies provides special challenges to health promotion campaign planners. This chapter examines how the message strategies and activities used in health promotion campaigns can be targeted to meet the needs of multicultural audiences.

In the final chapter, Chapter 7, of the book we review many of the major conclusions reached in the previous chapters. We identify relevant strategies for promoting effective multicultural health communication at each of the levels of communication examined. Specific suggestions are offered to help both health care providers and consumers use multicultural communication to enhance the quality of health care delivery.

2

Multicultural Communication and Personal Health

Ultimately,
You are the source of wellness—
Mind, body, and heart.

◆ Symbolic Aspects of Health and Illness

"Human illness is not only a physical condition but a symbolic one as well" (Barnlund, 1976, p. 718). What we experience as health or illness is based on the perceptual judgments we make about the relative quality of our physical and psychological condition. The meanings individuals assign to their health status are strongly influenced by their cultural backgrounds and experiences, and these culturally based meanings strongly influence the health care choices and decisions they make, their relative confidence in their health care providers and treatment regimen, and even their actual physical responses to health care treatment (Benson, 1979; Kreps, 1988b; Siegal, 1986). Although the use of prescription drugs, surgical procedures, and assorted health care therapies are the primary ways that the physical aspects of illness are treated, communication is the primary means by which the symbolic aspects of illness are influenced.

Health care treatment must attend to both the physical and symbolic aspects of illness to be effective. Enlightened health care practitioners communicate to learn about the different culturally based health beliefs, values, and attitudes that influence their clients' interpretations of health and health care (Becker, 1974). They communicate with their clients to elicit information about clients' symbolic interpretations of illness and to provide relevant information and feedback about these interpretations to help consumers make sense out of their health care (Kreps & Thornton, 1992).

Similarly, health care providers have their own symbolic interpretations of different health conditions. Clients with culturally stigmatized health conditions, such as AIDS and other sexually transmitted diseases, are likely to be treated quite differently by health care staff than are other consumers (Kreps, 1988b). In fact, there is widespread evidence that people with AIDS have faced blatant discrimination within the modern health care system (Johnson & Hopkins, 1990; Lambert, 1991; Mondragon, Kirkman-Liff, & Schneller, 1991; Strauss, Fagerhaugh, Suczek, & Weiner, 1991). Much of this discrimination is based on unrealistic fears, misunderstandings, and homophobia (Shilts, 1987; Treichler, 1987, 1988). There are powerful cultural influences on individual interpretations of and responses to health care. In this chapter, we examine the ways communication can influence the symbolic aspects of health and health care and how multicultural communication can influence personal health.

◆ Stress and Health

A captive audience client in a dentist's chair was listening as her dentist explained why she appeared to be so susceptible to cavities, even though she flossed, brushed, and rinsed and had a checkup every six months. "Your saliva is too acid," he explained. "You must be under a great deal of stress," he noted. She responded affirmatively with gargling sounds. She was in the process of preparing her dossier for promotion and tenure; she was preparing a grant proposal, not to mention teaching assignments and grading. Yes, she was under stress.

Stress factors can threaten the human body's immune system, increasing its vulnerability to psychological and physical pathologies. Investigations in biobehavioral science—a panoply of basic, applied, and clinical sciences that contribute to an understanding of behavior (Elliot, Hamburg, & Parton, 1982)—reveal that there is a significant correlation between stress and psychopathology as well as cancer and cardiovascular diseases. Dental surgeons indicate that cavities are not necessarily caused by the presence of bacteria that coexist in the human body along with other organisms but by the change in the pH balance of the saliva caused by stress.

The human body is exposed daily to bacteria, viruses, and conditions that are fraught with possibilities of infection. These multiple threats to human health are resisted through a variety of internal biological and psychological mechanisms. For example, it has been empirically verified that psychological variables such as feelings of physical well-being, control, and competence can help individuals resist and even overcome serious health threats such as cancer and cardiovascular disease (Benson, 1979; Cohen, Sullivan, & Branehog, 1988; Cousins, 1979; Greenfield, Kaplan, & Ware, 1985; Siegal, 1986). The intricate interactions between the human body and the many health-threatening stimuli that confront it illustrate the systems principles of *interdependence* (mutual influences between health threats and health preservation strategies), *interactiveness* (multiple influences on human health), and *homeostasis* (the body's attempts to maintain internal stability and balance).

◆ Culture Shock as a Form of Stress

A source of stress that influences mental health is *culture shock* associated with the mental and physical energy expended in adjusting to the changes and uncertainties of adapting to a new cultural group, whether it is an ethnic, professional, organizational, local, national, or international cultural group (Gudykunst & Kim, 1992; Kim, 1991). Culture shock can lead to "frustration, anger, alienation, depression, and other such reactions" (Condon & Yousef, 1975, p. 262). In the modern health care system, where participants are regularly forced to adapt to a wide range of different national, ethnic, and professional cultures, health care providers and consumers are likely to experience high levels of stress, and as we already have mentioned, too much stress can be physically and mentally debilitating.

Whenever an individual needs to adapt to extraordinary changes—such as a new job, a new organization, a divorce, or a death—he or she pays a price physically, mentally, and emotionally. This is especially true for hospitalized consumers of health care who have to adapt to the bureaucracy of modern health care delivery systems, are separated from their normal "healthy" professional role, and must adopt a limited-potential *sick role* that is often extremely stressful (Crane, 1975; Kreps & Thornton, 1992). Health care consumers' abilities to engage in effective multicultural communication with the many different individuals they encounter in the modern health care system will help them overcome the limitations imposed by the sick role through establishing meaningful and supportive interpersonal relationships, eliciting cooperation from relevant others, and gathering pertinent information to enable them to actively participate in directing their health care.

Festinger's (1957) *cognitive dissonance theory* provides theoretical support for the physiological and psychological influences of culture shock. Cognitive dissonance is the tendency individuals have to change either their beliefs or behaviors to avoid the feeling of psychological discomfort known as *dissonance* (caused by any recognized inconsistencies in a person's beliefs and behaviors). Dissonance is similar to hunger; it is an aversive drive that motivates individuals to act in certain ways to avoid unpleasant feelings (Griffin, 1991). Dissonance, like culture shock, has negative influences on individual health.

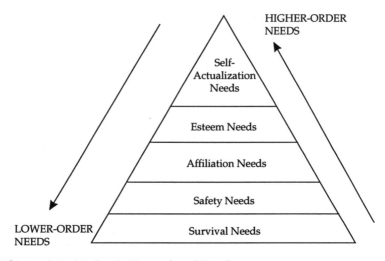

Figure 2.1. Maslow's Hierarchy of Needs

Dissonance could be represented as a separate layer on *Maslow's hierarchy of needs*, because dissonance acts as a psychological state, drive, need, or tension, similar to the primary human needs Maslow identifies in his model (Maslow, 1943; 1954). Maslow's model suggests that human beings are driven to satisfy a series of five successive levels of individual needs (see Figure 2.1 for a depiction of Maslow's hierarchy of needs).

Human behavior can be explained by identifying the specific need level an individual is in the process of fulfilling. When the most basic of all needs, *survival needs*, are satisfied, human beings become interested in safety needs. When survival and safety needs are met, then human beings become concerned with affiliation needs. Once survival, safety, and affiliation needs are met, people become concerned with addressing their need for respect and *esteem*. Finally, when these first four levels of needs are satisfied, people then become interested in achieving their needs for personal fulfillment and growth, something Maslow referred to as *self-actualization*. The need to avoid dissonance is also a basic human need, perhaps one that might be placed right after the need for safety and before the need for affiliation on Maslow's hierarchy.

Ineffective multicultural relations often lead to psychological discomfort and dissonance, violating our basic need to avoid such psychological states. To avoid such discomfort, individuals need to develop comfortable and satisfying multicultural relations, especially in the modern health care system where multicultural relations are an inherent feature. Effective multicultural relations can help members of the health care community resist the stressors that are likely to derive from working interdependently with so many individuals representing different cultural groups. By avoiding the dissonance and stress caused by tense multicultural relations in health care contexts, individuals are able to help balance their complex body chemistry, protecting their physical and psychological health. In this way, effective multicultural communication acts to promote personal health.

An example of culture shock on the national level may be a councilman who is elected to the U.S. Senate and takes his family to the nation's capital. There are an incredible number of adjustments to make, not only on the part of the senator but also on the part of the spouse and the children. Gearing up to live in a new city calls for adjusting to all levels of needs—physical, social, intellectual, and emotional.

At the international level the efforts take on an even greater magnitude. A communications professional who was employed by an international organization in Geneva, Switzerland, discussed his experience with culture shock at great length. The professional and his family could not afford the high-priced homes in Geneva, so they settled on the Swiss border near France. This area was picturesque, but the commuting time was quite long. "Even ordinary things like doing your laundry were so complicated," he complained. "The washing machines don't operate like the American ones, and it takes twice as long." He also complained about the way the workday was divided into two parts, broken up by two-hour lunch breaks. "I'd rather work for eight hours and go home," he explained. "And drinking wine at noon!"

Although multicultural relations are an inherent part of the modern health care system, culture shock is not an inevitability. Culture shock is most likely to occur when individuals are not sensitive to cultural differences, do not learn about different cultural norms and mores, and do not develop the abilities to adapt to the different culturally distinct individuals they encounter in health care systems. Development of communication attitudes and skills that demonstrate an appreciation of and sensitivity to cultural diversity will enable participants in the modern health care system to avoid the many physical and psychological perils associated with culture shock.

◆ Prevention Model

Proficiency in multicultural communication is a major coping factor in managing stress (Albee & Joffe, 1977). Albee (1982a; 1982b; 1985a; 1985b; 1985c; 1988), in the model for the prevention of *psychopathology*, used the analogy of a fraction, with *stress factors* as the numerator and *coping factors* as the denominator (see Table 2.1 for a depiction of the model for preventing psychopathology). As coping factors (in the denominator) increase, the stress factors (in the numerator) decrease. Conversely, the fewer coping skills one has the greater the amount of stress there is. There are many situations that contribute to stress—ineffective communication, change, uncertainty, financial problems, relationship problems, employment problems, and environmental problems. However, as the model depicted in Table 2.1 points out, coping factors can work to decrease the stress factors. Coping factors include supportive relationships, economic assistance, education, preventive health care, and communication skills.

Multicultural communication proficiency, as a main coping factor in this model, facilitates the achievement of objectives toward the enhancement of personal health through these skills:

TABLE 2.1 Model for the Prevention of Psychopathology

Stress Factors (numerator)	Communication Deficiency Change, Uncertainty Financial Problems Relationship Problems Employment Problems Environmental Problems
Coping Factors (denominator)	Communication Proficiency Financial Assistance Support Systems Preventive Health Care Education

SOURCE: Model adapted from G. W. Albee (1985), *The primary prevention of psychopathology* (Lecture presented at the University of Hawaii School of Medicine).

1. Accessing, processing, disseminating and evaluating information
2. Managing feelings and attitudes
3. Acquiring competent intercultural skills and behaviors

This proficiency enables one to communicate effectively with people of different backgrounds in expressing one's needs, to learn about others, and to adapt to the many constraints of life. It enables one to obtain information from health care providers and professionals in diverse cultural settings. It enables one to develop and reinforce interpersonal relationships and to build a supportive climate in new situations. It enables one to acquire skills and behaviors that would enhance both mental and physical health (Kunimoto, 1977). This prevention model is appropriate for all participants in the modern health care system—health care providers, consumers and their loved ones, and support staff.

◆ Multicultural Communication Proficiency

Proficiency in multicultural communication may be described as skills in communicating with members of diverse cultural groups to achieve desired objectives. Combining the definitions of *group* and *culture* by Brislin (1981) and Geertz (1973) provides the description of a culture as an identifiable group whose members operate on the assumptions that they share beliefs, experiences, and patterns of meanings. When two different groups work together, they are participating in intercultural communication. The smallest intercultural group is a dyad.

Organizational theorists (Trice & Beyer, 1984) state that culture has two basic components: (1) its substance, or the network of meanings contained in its ideologies, norms, and values; and (2) its forms, or the practices whereby these meanings are expressed, affirmed, and communicated to members. For example, the Hawaiian culture embraces the concept of *ohana*, the extended family. The members of the *ohana* consist of not only blood relatives but also friends who share the same values and work together for a common good. Many groups in Hawaii who share similar values have joined in an *ohana* that has gained in strength politically. This collective spirit of *ohana* clearly exemplifies the effective use of multicultural communication to build meaningful interpersonal relationships and establish solidarity among individuals from disparate cultural orientations and backgrounds.

◆ Communication Proficiency and Empowerment

Whether a health care professional is serving a client in a dyad or in small groups such as a family group, or accessing information from another department or agency, he or she is participating in intercultural communication. Whether the desired result is information-gain, attitude-change and/or reinforcement, or skill-acquisition, intercultural communication skills are imperative.

Whether a patient is seeking information for prevention, enhancement, or a cure, the ability to access information, persuade others, and participate in the selection of one's own protocols is mandatory. Intercultural communication proficiency empowers one in the decision-making processes of personal health.

◆ In-House Stress and Burnout

Health care professionals themselves often experience *burnout* even as they care for their patients (Maslach, 1982). Burnout is a cacophony of different experiences and powerful emotions, where an individual's joy and inspiration for work and life are replaced by feelings of indifference and submission (Dass & Gorman, 1985). Stress from unsuccessful efforts to adapt to uncertainty and change, rather than from physical exhaustion itself, appears to be a main cause of burnout (Miller, Stiff, & Ellis, 1988; Ray, 1987).

◆ Case Study of the Influence of Stress on a Provider's Health

A Japanese-American registered nurse (RN) was promoted to be the supervisor of a ward of registered nurses and licensed practical nurses (LPNs) of multi-ethnic backgrounds at a private geriatric center in Hawaii. (RNs receive significantly more training and usually have broader health care responsibilities, such as drawing blood and administering medications, than licensed practical nurses). Although she was pleased at receiving the promotion, which meant greater financial rewards and control, she also felt as though she was given a heavy burden that caused her migraine headaches and a queasy feeling in her stomach. Her licensed practical nurses were primarily immigrant Filipinas who seemed to resent her promotion and were uncooperative, asking for shifts to be rescheduled, calling in sick, and not carrying out their duties promptly.

She was at the point of seriously considering asking for a transfer, a young Filipina woman whom she had befriended and advised in earning her LPN certification a year ago, extended her support. The Filipina LPN was running a foster care home for elderly patients, and the supervisor had given her encouragement in this endeavor as well as in her earning her certificate. The LPN explained to her that some Filipino immigrants retained hostility toward the Japanese because of the Japanese occupation of the Philippines during World War II. She explained that the Filipinos were generally a group that expressed nurturing behavior, especially toward the elderly, and were respectful toward persons in positions of authority.

This LPN happened to be held in high regard by hospital social workers, who referred their difficult long-term care patients to her. The social workers trusted her so that they would ask her to take in difficult patients who had been refused by other caregivers. For several years she had cared for an elderly Caucasian woman whose temperament alienated her only daughter as well as her foster home caregivers. An elderly Korean woman diagnosed as having Alzheimer's disease was sent to her. The woman was ambulatory and could talk coherently, often demanding her meals immediately after she had eaten. Several times instead of using the commode, she defecated into a dinner plate and brought it to her caregiver. In time she began to use the commode, ate fairly regularly, and became more manageable.

Her children visited her a half-dozen times a year, mostly only on holidays, such as Mother's Day. However, the elderly woman excused them by saying, "They are so busy." This woman lived in the LPN's home for five years. Recently, the social workers placed an elderly movie personality in the LPN's home. This woman is surrounded by pictures of famous movie stars with whom she used to work. She and the other elderly woman live in a unit attached to the main house, and they are included as family members and attended to by the LPN's two children and husband.

The LPN serendipitously began her career as operator of a foster care home when she was a newlywed from the Philippines and a social worker was having difficulty placing an elderly married couple who needed health care. Even though they had not intended to provide such services, the LPN and her husband accepted the responsibility because the couple was desperate. The couple lived with them for 10 years before they moved in with relatives. They were treated as family and were regarded by the Filipino couple's children as grandparents.

The LPN communicated privately with the nursing supervisor and listened to her while she expressed her concerns about the lack of cooperation from the Filipina nurses and LPNs. The LPN told her that she was her advocate and would speak to the group. Meanwhile, the supervisor attended several training sessions on intercultural communication. At the training sessions she received feedback on her communication style, mostly on nonverbal messages: eye contact, facial expression, and paralanguage. She participated in dyadic exercises in which her partner monitored her nonverbal messages regarding dichotomies of friendliness versus unfriendliness; egalitarianism versus authoritativeness; caring versus uncaring; genuine versus insincere; patient versus impatient; and warm versus cold. The exercises revealed that she could produce more positive results monitoring her paralanguage and body language. With the LPN as mediator and her improved nonverbal communication skills she was able to improve the relationship between herself and the Filipina health care workers. Her stress was under control, and she was able to enhance her personal health as well as her services to the elderly.

◆ Professional Vulnerability

In a health enhancement center a health care professional with an overload of cases was heard running around saying, "Here we are dealing with prevention, and no one seems to know that I'm having a nervous breakdown." Professionals, in dealing with their clients, often work to send their best communication messages to them both verbally and nonverbally. With their colleagues, however, because of their perception of one another as professionals who do not need to be treated as clients, and because of time constraints, they tend to overlook many of the components of building a supportive climate for one another (Marshall, 1980; Ray, 1987).

◆ A Case Study

In a health enhancement center in a Western state, a concerted effort was made to emphasize prevention of pathology,
utilizing the services of a team of doctors, nurses, psychologists, nutritionists, and kinesiologists. The prevention center
was housed in a modern structure also occupied by affluent,
elderly retirees. The retirees had signed a contract to live there
for an extended period; they had their meals served in an elabo-
rate dining room, and a director of recreation supervised their
entertainment. The prevention program was affiliated with
faculty and staff at the university and the university hospital and
was in the process of building its own complex, having leased
several floors of the building for its purposes. The prevention
program participants lived for a month, the duration of the
program, in the same building as the elderly residents. Except
for sharing the building space, the residents and the participants lived separate lives. The participants had their own dining room where menus included foods that were low in sodium
and fats and high in complex carbohydrates and fiber. They also
attended lectures on nutrition, stress management, cardiovascular diseases, diabetes, and exercise presented by nutritionists,
psychologists, doctors, and kinesiologists. They went on health
walks outdoors as well as worked out in their exercise room.

For all practical purposes, the residents and participants
could have been regarded as members of two different cultural
groups. The genteel, elderly residents occasionally expressed
their resentment in sharing elevators and lounges with the
participants, who were usually dressed in jogging suits and
conducted themselves in a robust manner. The health care
professionals (who commuted from a nearby hospital) interacted only with the participants, not with the residents. The
climate was one of constrained coexistence. Furthermore, in a
survey measuring stress levels of professionals and participants,
both groups responded that they were experiencing stress,
with the participants indicating a significantly higher level than
the professionals.

Intercultural communication training was introduced to the prevention program as an intervention to create a more conducive climate in the health enhancement center as well as within the residential complex itself. The professional team and the participants were trained in separate sessions consisting of presentations explaining the rationale for sensitive and caring intercultural communication, monitoring of the cultural climate through reflective listening and empathy, transmitting appropriate verbal and nonverbal messages, and evaluating the results of the intercultural interaction.

The training program included enactive situations, such as role-playing and dyadic exercises in the transmission and interpretation of body language and paralanguage. Exercises in reflective listening provided training in monitoring the attitudes and feelings of others and in responding empathetically. The culmination of the training program was a social event planned by the participants, "Aloha: An Evening in Hawaii," to which the elderly residents were invited.

The participants dressed in improvised Hawaiian attire and danced their version of the hula, led the entire assembly in community singing, and ended the evening by presenting leis, anthuriums, and dendrobium orchids to the elderly residents while singing, "For You a Lei." When the fresh flowers ran out the participants gave away their cellophane leis to the residents, and these were also received with enthusiasm.

There was a significant difference in the climate of the residential complex following the event. The participants, the medical team, and the residents interacted affably in the building and in the community. Participants noted that the elderly residents smiled at them in the elevators and the lounges and pointed them out as "stars" when they met them outdoors on their walks.

In a pre- and post-training survey, members of the medical team and participants indicated a decrease in the perception scores of their own stress levels and an increase in their perception of self-esteem and communication proficiency. At a general meeting, the director of the prevention center announced that the social event to which the residents were invited was the first combined event since the center was established two years earlier and that it seemed to have enhanced the relationships among the participants, residents, and professionals. A positive outcome of the training program was the transference of the positive regard of the residents to the incoming group of new participants to the center's program.

◆ Communicator as Change Agent

Participants in intercultural interactions generally operate within time constraints, without the benefit of extensive ethnographic studies of the groups involved. Whether one is a professional or a client, the communicator often has a limited time frame in which to create a milieu in which there is a synchrony of meanings to bring about mutually desired outcomes.

The communicator behaves as a change agent during the intercultural interaction, monitoring the situation by obtaining data through observation, reflective listening, and empathy, using this information to transmit appropriate verbal and nonverbal messages to empower relational partners to produce mutually desired results in health management.

◆ Self-Esteem and Stress Management

The ability to communicate effectively seems to produce an increase of self-esteem in many persons (Bolton, 1986). Often, improved acceptance of oneself is derived from training in communication skills. College students who completed training programs in intercultural communication had significantly higher scores in their perception of self-esteem and confidence in facing change and uncertainty. They also reported in a follow-up study that in subsequent classes and projects they were able to initiate communication with their classmates and create a context that enabled them to achieve results synergistically—from group projects to studying for examinations (Kunimoto, 1977).

One's personality development and mental and physical health are linked to the caliber of one's communication. Conversely, lack of communication or frequent exposure to poor communication diminishes one both emotionally and physically (Bolton, 1986). Often, improved self-esteem is derived from training in intercultural communication skills. The ability to communicate effectively, interculturally, seems to produce increased self-esteem in many persons, enabling them to create a milieu that enhances their personal health. Improvements in self-esteem will also have inevitable positive influences on individuals' symbolic interpretations of their health condition and control over their health care.

◆ Alternative Perspectives on Health Care

With health costs spiraling out of control, the U.S. Congress recently appropriated $2 million to establish the Office of Alternative Medicine at the National Institutes of Health. It aims to bring traditional and nontraditional communities together and will put therapies such as massage techniques and herbal medicines under scientific scrutiny.

Most practitioners of *alternative medicine* advocate self-help, understanding that a person's attitude, emotional outlook, and lifestyle are as important as identifying and combating the illness itself, clearly recognizing the important influences of the symbolic aspects of illness on individual health. When the coauthor from Hawaii had a persistent cough, she went to a clinic to her internist. She was then referred to specialists from one department to another—ear-nose-throat, pulmonary surgery, and allergy. X-rays of her chest and sinuses revealed no evidence of tuberculosis or sinusitis. A series of tests for allergies was found to be negative. A bronchoscopy revealed no evidence of pathology. The doctors assured her that she was fortunate that she had nothing serious—no cancer, no tuberculosis, no allergy, no sinusitis. She would just have to live with the annoying cough and cope with sprays and lozenges.

After "coping" for most of the academic year—coughing every 15 minutes day and night and keeping her husband awake many nights—out of desperation she decided to try an alternative medical therapy recommended by her friends—kiate nerve therapy, a Japanese massage therapy. She had hesitated for a long time previously, because this was a long-term (six months) program not covered by health insurance.

The therapist informed her that her persistent cough was the result of an immune system that was weakened by a lifestyle that included going without sleep for days when completing projects, eating excessive amounts of refined sugar (she is a confirmed chocoholic), and maintaining a diet lacking in vital nutrients such as calcium. She was suffering from pinched nerves, the beginnings of osteoporosis, and a deteriorating muscle mass.

At the kiate clinic she encountered patients who were professionals, who, like her, had sought out the therapist after trying all the traditional practitioners (who were covered by health insurance). Having received no relief, in desperation they came to this therapist and were already experiencing greatly improved health.

Within a few weeks of treatments the author's cough disappeared, and her friends also noticed that the excessive eye-blinking habit that she had since her college days had disappeared. She was rapidly approaching her ideal weight, and her colleagues remarked that she was looking more youthful. She did have one setback. After a month of treatment, she got overcomplacent and ate six rich chocolate truffles in one afternoon. She started to cough again, although not as frequently or severely. After she began to cut down on her sugar intake her coughing stopped. As soon as she deviates from healthful habits by eating excessive sugar, cutting down on her sleep, or overeating at a buffet brunch, she begins to cough.

She has since learned to listen to her body and monitors her activities to cut down on stress. Her improved health has so impressed her husband, who was skeptical at first, that both he and his sister have enrolled in the program and have experienced improved health. His sister's arthritis and tinnitus disappeared within two weeks.

The author is now in her third month of therapy, and she is looking forward to gaining greater strength and gearing toward optimal health and greater productivity. Her friend, a former nurse who had a mastectomy and found that cancer had spread to her lungs a year later, not only underwent chemotherapy but attended the American Nurses' Holistic Association conference and participated in holistic therapies such as massage, meditation, visualization, acupressure, and healing by contact. An X-ray taken shortly after the conference revealed that the cancerous nodes had disappeared.

The director of the Office of Alternative Medicine, Joe Jacobs, MD, is understandably excited about the promise of unconventional treatments. "All of a sudden, we've increased our understanding of what can help people," he has said (Gill, 1993, p. 64). Since many alternative therapies are rooted in different ethnic, racial, national, and religious cultures, it is a sign of multicultural respect and sensitivity to acknowledge the legitimacy and potential efficacy of such approaches to health care. The failure of many members of the traditional Western health care system, including the vast majority of companies providing health insurance, to recognize and sanction such treatments is a clear expression of ethnocentrism. Progressive health care consumers and providers do not prejudicially limit their examination and selection of health care treatments based on ethnocentrism, but endeavor to review the wide range of traditional and alternative courses of treatment available, enabling them to determine the best therapies for the individual health care problems they are attempting to address.

3

Relational Multicultural Communication in Health Care

Communicating
In-tune-ness or what-a-mess
Depends on dyads.

◆ Interpersonal Relations

People develop interpersonal relationships to establish and maintain social agreements for interacting with one another in cooperative and coordinated ways. The interpersonal relationship is the basic building block of social organization (Kreps, 1990a). We provide our relational partners with a wide range of services and support, such as friendship, love, caring, feedback, and help in the accomplishment of instrumental goals.

We have numerous interpersonal relationships in our personal and professional lives. These relationships range in their development from incipient (just beginning) to intimate. Many of our business and acquaintance relationships stay at a rather superficial incipient level of development, where we have few expectations for one another. Other relationships are quite intense and intimate, where we have many expectations for each other's behaviors.

All relationships are based on the development and maintenance of *implicit contracts*, mutually understood agreements to meet each one's, often unspoken, expectations for the other (Kreps & Thornton, 1992; Rossiter & Pearce, 1975). In incipient relationships these implicit contracts are few and are generally quite rudimentary. For example, you probably have some basic expectations that when you are out shopping any clerks in the store will treat you civilly and fairly and the clerks probably expect the same general behaviors from you. These basic expectations are largely determined by cultural *norms* for *role performances*. In different *cultural milieus* (settings) there are likely to be different expectations for such behaviors. Therefore, an understanding of the fundamental cultural norms operating in different social settings is essential to meeting even the basic incipient expectations for relational cooperation.

It takes a good deal more time and effort to develop intimate interpersonal relationships because of the many implicit contracts governing how relational partners are expected to interact and cooperate. In intimate relationships we learn over time to fulfill the many, often subtle, expectations we have for each other. Through the *norm of reciprocity*, which encourages individuals to respond in kind to one another, relational partners are encouraged to reciprocate with one another when their expectations are met. As more expectations are met and implicit contracts are established, the intimacy of an interpersonal relationship grows. This is known as the process of *relationship development*. When individuals fail to meet relational expectations, the norm of reciprocity encourages reciprocal violations of expectations, leading to a process of *relationship deterioration*.

Furthermore, individual expectations and cultural norms for role performances are *emergent phenomena* (are continually changing), necessitating periodic updates in implicit contracts over time. To maintain effective interpersonal relationships, then, you must use interpersonal communication to continually identify your relational partners' different and emergent expectations, to let relational partners know that you intend to meet those expectations, and to share your expectations with your relational partners.

◆ Interpersonal Relations in Health Care

Interpersonal relationships are central to the provision of health care. Consumers and providers must establish clear implicit contracts for coordinating activities in the health care enterprise. Interdependent health care providers, as well as health care system support staff, also depend on developing cooperative relationships.

An important challenge to the development of effective health care relationships is the ability to bridge cultural differences between health care providers and their clients. Physicians appear to be looking for effective ways of eliciting patient concerns and improving patient satisfaction with their medical treatment to prevent malpractice suits and to feel better about their own work (Wyatt, 1991). Professionals in a dominant culture who lack multicultural communication proficiency may tend to misperceive a minority or culturally different client (Sodowsky & Taffe, 1991). Health care professionals are acknowledging the urgency of attending to the relational component of the provider-patient context. In this chapter we present a conceptual framework for relational multicultural communication exemplified by case studies and suggest a course of action in developing proficiency in establishing sensitive and effective multicultural health care provider-consumer relationships.

◆ Uncertainty Reduction in Relational Communication

In Chapter 2, we described the relationship between multicultural communication proficiency and personal health. The greater the number of diverse groups one can communicate with successfully to achieve results in information gain, attitude change or reinforcement, and skill acquisition or behavior change, the greater the reduction in uncertainty and stress (Gudykunst, 1988).

Despite evidence of the low risk of occupational exposure to AIDS (Acquired Immune Deficiency Syndrome), many health care workers' behavior demonstrates a high fear of contagion (Johnson & Hopkins, 1990; Lambert, 1991). Multicultural education, along with relevant and accurate information about AIDS, was recommended to decrease providers' unrealistic fears of contagion (Heisenhelder & LaCharite, 1989).

Gudykunst and his colleagues have pursued a research program of testing and extending *uncertainty reduction theory* in the context of intercultural communication (Gudykunst, 1988; 1993). Noteworthy are five new hypotheses regarding uncertainty reduction in encounters between *high-* and *low-context cultures*:

1. Uncertainty differs in high- and low-context cultures. Uncertainty reduction in high-context cultures (as in Japanese) involves predicting whether strangers will follow *group* or cultural norms. In low-context cultures (as in American) uncertainty reduction involves predicting *individual* behavior.

2. Members of high-context cultures focus on predicting adherence to norms when speaking their native language; when speaking *English*, they try to predict *individual* behavior, just as a low-context native English speaker would.

3. Knowing someone's background or having mutual friends may reduce uncertainty for members of high-context cultures. Therefore, not having contact with strangers' communication networks before the initial interaction increases uncertainty for high-context cultures, but not for low-context cultures in which norms provide much less information.

4. Being unable to empathize with strangers will increase uncertainty in high-context cultures, but not in low-context cultures.

5. Lack of knowledge about a stranger's background will increase uncertainty in high-context cultures, but not in low-context cultures.

◆ Overcoming Cancer: A Case Study

The Chinese-American engineer's face was familiar to cancer patients in a California hospital. He had overcome testicular cancer after he had been given a massive dose of an experimental drug. Now as a volunteer in oncology wards and hospices he talked to cancer patients, many of whom were diagnosed as being terminally ill. As he approached the bedside of a young Hawaii-born Japanese-American executive who had recently undergone surgery for testicular cancer, the patient's eyes widened with dread. He had equated the presence of the man who visited terminal patients in hospices and oncology wards with his own death sentence.

The executive's face blanched as he recognized the volunteer. "I guess my case is hopeless if you're here," he said. "On the contrary," replied the volunteer, "I'm here to give you hope." He explained that when he himself was debilitated by cancer and had shrunk to a weight of 85 pounds, his doctor had given him a massive dose of an experimental drug and he had survived. More volunteers were needed to test the drug, and he urged the patient to participate in the experiment.

The executive agreed to be one of the subjects in the experiment. "You'll be one of the dots on the chart," he was told by the doctor who was the project director. "We hope that you will be one of those who experiences complete remission." The doctor also proceeded to explain some of the negative aspects of the treatment: nausea, hearing loss, and baldness (hopefully, temporary).

Several months later the executive was in remission. During his treatments the president of his corporation encouraged his staff to give the young man support and assured him of job security. When the remission of his cancer was announced, the president gave a celebration dinner to which the doctor, with whom the executive had developed a close relationship, was invited.

Eight months later, however, tests revealed a recurrence of cancer in his system. The engineer/volunteer who had been given a massive dose of the drug several years ago, however, had showed no sign of recurrence. Both the executive and his doctor questioned whether the protocols had been aggressive enough. The doctor sent him to a university hospital that was testing another experimental drug. This time the protocol was successful, and 10 years later, the executive—now vice-president of a growing Western corporation—has been pronounced cured. The executive and the doctor who initially treated him have maintained their relationship throughout the years, and recently when the doctor and his family visited Hawaii, they were taken to a luau by the executive's family.

The foregoing is among many of the case studies that can be compiled by a researcher gathering data on the ethnography of health communication with a major focus on relational multicultural communication. Although the outcomes for this case were felicitous, there were many moments interspersed with problems that would engage the interest of any communication scholar.

For example, when the executive experienced a recurrence of the cancer, some of his family members in Hawaii questioned the choice of protocol. Some members indicated their preference for using healing herbs and Eastern approaches, such as meditation, rather than strong experimental drugs. In the end, however, the executive, who was a graduate in mathematics from Stanford University and who embraced the Western tradition of scientific inquiry, prevailed. He said that he preferred to risk the experimental treatment at the university hospital rather than undertake the Eastern approaches. Furthermore, he emphasized, he had great confidence in the professionals in the medical field and their methods. In addition, he insisted on knowing all aspects of his illness and treatment, including the side effects and his chances of survival. He saw accessing information as a means of reducing uncertainty, a source of stress.

His doctor complied by providing medical data that his patient requested. He and his patient agreed on the type of treatment. The patient's mother tearfully agreed to accept whatever protocol the patient selected. Today she says that she is grateful that her son made the choice—the right choice. Her son confirms that his doctor had *empowered* him by enabling him to provide input toward the health care decision-making process.

By contrast, a 34-year-old female patient in Japan who was dying of cancer was not told of her illness by the doctor. Three reasons were given to explain why Japanese physicians often do not disclose a patient's terminal condition or answer specific questions about the diagnosis (Takahashi, 1990). These are (1) avoidance of patient distress, (2) reluctance to destroy the relationship of interdependence, and (3) the physician's own anxiety or fear (Takahashi, 1990). Her American counterpart, the executive, who could have been dying of cancer over a decade ago, was empowered by his doctor, who gave him information and a choice of taking an experimental drug, which eventually cured him.

◆ Multiple Health Care Relationships

During his 2-year treatment the executive developed relationships with a host of health care professionals—some for a brief moment and others for a longer period. His initial oncologist, who was also the project director of the first protocol, was the person with whom he maintained the longest and most intimate professional relationship. He depended on the oncologist to provide him with full and accurate information about treatment options, and the oncologist fulfilled these expectations. The oncologist expected his patient to carefully evaluate treatment options and trust him to provide good medical advice. Patient and provider met each other's expectations and established effective implicit contracts.

Several other interpersonal relationships were established with members of the health care staff. For example, the head nurse who was the main information channel, the nurses who administered the drugs intravenously, the technicians who tested him, and the nurses in the ward who attended to his needs were all important parts of his health care system—a multicultural system that called for relational communication proficiency on the part of professionals and the patient. It was multicultural communication proficiency that led to decision making in selecting different forms of treatment. It was this proficiency that helped influence the values and attitudes of patient, family members, and professionals and the behaviors of the persons in the health care environment.

We saw in the Prevention Model in Chapter 2 that relational health increases the development of support systems and decreases stress factors that undermine physical and mental health. Relational health is a function of multicultural communication proficiency, a successful interaction between intrapersonal and interpersonal communication.

Intrapersonal communication refers to the individual level and to the messages that are being created and interpreted by the individual. Intrapersonal influences in the foregoing case study are exemplified by the cancer patient wondering what his chances for survival were, his friend the doctor wondering whether he had undertreated his patient the first time and if this had led to the recurrence of cancer, and his mother who thought that her son should be treated by Eastern techniques and healing herbs. Each of these intrapersonal messages is affected by cultural variables such as health beliefs, cultural expectations, and worldviews.

The cancer survivor's cultural worldview was different from that of his Japanese ancestors. It was one of individualism rather than collectivism and self-control rather than fatalism. He elected to participate in an aggressive, experimental treatment of cancer rather than the gentler mode of using herbs and meditation as suggested by his mother.

In light of the successful treatment of his illness and his being free of cancer for 10 years, it appears that he made the best health care choice and exemplifies what researchers are calling *personal communication worldview* (Dodd, 1991). He tended to organize information about himself and utilize a communication style that reflected his fundamental views toward the amount of control he perceived. For example, he chose his treatment style in consultation with his oncologist. His demeanor and composure as well as the ability to establish a relationship that facilitated interaction with his doctor enabled him to access information on state-of-the-art treatments as well as to provide input to his doctor on his choice of treatment. Reciprocally, the doctor empowered his patient by listening to him and providing information, thus reducing uncertainty and stress.

Although this executive was generally task-oriented rather than people-oriented—to the dismay of his mother, who emphasized relationships with people—his interaction with people produced optimal results. For example, whenever he went in for intravenous administration of the experimental drugs, he felt inordinate discomfort. However, he did not call the nurse incessantly to complain but rather "saved" her services for when he seriously needed her. In this way, he explained to his family, he would maintain a more positive relationship for the duration of his treatment.

The family members, who flew in from Hawaii to California to visit him during his ordeal, brought orchids and Hawaiian candies and macadamia nuts for his doctors, nurses, and attendants and for fellow patients in the oncology ward. Although a certain amount of grimness prevailed in a ward where patients died with some degree of predictability, on these occasions the climate was one of positive regard, and the spirit of *aloha* reigned.

◆ Content and Relationship Communication

Intercultural communication has both *content* and *relationship dimensions*; that is, every time we communicate with another we provide each other with both content information about conversational topics and relationship information about the nature of our relationship with each other (Watzlawick, Beavin, & Jackson, 1967). Communication, and ultimately meaning, is cemented with the two essential notions of content and relationship. Our relationship with the person with whom we are communicating affects how the message is interpreted. Messages also influence the development and interpretation of relationships.

Often people are so concerned about crafting the content of their messages, they neglect monitoring and controlling the relational aspects of their communication, especially since relational messages define the relationship being developed between interactants. In fact, every time you say something to someone else you have a potential positive or negative influence on the development of your relationship with them. Messages that violate others' cultural expectations provide relational information that will inevitably lead to relational deterioration because these messages demonstrate a lack of respect for relational partners, whereas messages that *validate* others' cultural expectations enhance relationship development.

Relational messages vary in quality, ranging on a continuum from *personal messages* to *object messages* (Kreps & Thornton, 1992). (See Figure 3.1 for a model depicting the *personal-object communication continuum.*) On one end of the continuum is personal communication, which validates the individuality of others by demonstrating respect for them. Personal communication does not mean always agreeing with others, but it does mean that you show respect and a willingness to be influenced by others. On the other end of the continuum is object communication, which demonstrates a lack of respect and concern for the individuality of the other person. It is dehumanizing and facilitates relationship deterioration. Personal communication satisfies the cultural expectations of relational others. Object communication tends to violate cultural expectations, failing to satisfy implicit contracts and retarding relational development. Therefore, it is important to use personal

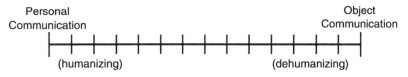

Figure 3.1. Continuum of Personal-Object Communication

SOURCE: Reprinted by permission of Waveland Press, Inc. from Gary L. Kreps and Barbara C. Thornton, *Health Communication: Theory and Practice, Second Edition*, p. 24. Copyright © 1992 by Waveland Press, Inc, Prospect Heights, Illinois.

communication in health care relationships to promote multicultural relationship development and enhance cooperation.

Verbal and nonverbal messages by health care providers can make a significant impact on patients as well as friends and relatives. Verbal messages tend to be best suited to conveying content information ("Just the facts, Ma'am"), whereas nonverbal messages are best suited for conveying relational information. Nonverbal messages such as body language, facial expression, eye contact, gestures, posture, paralanguage intonation, and volume, rate, and timbre of speech often accentuate and clarify verbal messages, helping relational others interpret the relationship implications of what is said.

Although nonverbal messages often clarify verbal messages, sometimes, when verbal and nonverbal systems are not used together effectively, they confuse communication. For example, an aide was reprimanded by a nurse for conveying an emergency message in a leisurely manner, creating confusion. The nonverbal messages she used did not match the urgency of the content information that should have been expressed. Sometimes the failure to articulate the use of verbal and nonverbal messages can cause relational difficulties in health care. When the executive, in the case described earlier in this chapter, checked out of the hospital after one of his treatments, a friend called the hospital and asked for him. When the receptionist informed him, in a rather solemn tone, "He's gone," meaning that he had checked out of the hospital, his friend thought that he had died and burst out crying.

◆ Dimensions of Interpersonal Relations

Dimensions of interpersonal relations include three types of message exchange patterns (Infante, 1988): control, trust, and intimacy. Control is measured by redundancy (how much change there is in the relational partner's negotiation over rights), dominance (how much one relational partner dominates the interaction), and power (the potential to influence or restrict a relational partner's behaviors). In some situations we need to control others; in other situations we need to have others exert control over us (Schutz, 1958).

Trust requires both members of a relationship to be trusting and trustworthy. By trusting, people admit that they are dependent on each other and that each believes the partner will not exploit the other or take advantage of the other's trust. Trust is not easy to establish. We trust others when they demonstrate to us that they respect us and will act in responsible ways towards us (Kreps, 1990a). One violation of relational expectations can destroy our trust in others and it may take a very long time, if ever, to reestablish that level of trust.

Intimacy measures how often partners use the other to confirm their feelings of separateness or connectedness in the relationship. The more connected the relationship, the more intimate the interpersonal relation is. Intimate relationships have well-developed implicit contracts in which members demonstrate their willingness to live up to each other's expectations.

In multicultural communication, information theory leads us to conclude that predictability is an important aspect of developing and maintaining effective relationships (Gudykunst, 1988). Interpersonal interactants seem to need a certain amount of redundancy in communication to increase predictability, reduce entropy, and help them maintain a comfortable psychological state.

Some ambiguities, however, occur in all communication relationships. The ambiguity is lessened by some normative areas of predictability within our own cultures. We implicitly understand communication rules if we share the same culture, and the job of decoding and interpreting the other person's messages is significantly easier. The ambiguity increases dramatically when we are interacting multiculturally. When we are not sharing the same cultural rules there are significantly more possible behaviors.

◆ Long-Distance Advocacy
   for an Aging Parent: A Case Study

Thousands of miles away in Connecticut, the daughter exhaled with relief as the social worker in Honolulu told her that they were able to get her father enrolled in an adult day care center and that her mother would finally be able to get some respite. The daughter, a professional of English-Irish descent, had felt helpless for months when she first heard from her mother in Hawaii that her father was diagnosed as having Alzheimer's disease. Her parents had bought a unit in a private care complex for the elderly several years ago when her father had retired, and their lives appeared to be filled with halcyon days.

About 18 months previously, however, her father began accusing people of taking his things—his wallet, his keys, and finally, his car. He was unable to find his car several times when he drove to the doctor or to the mall. When his wife took him to their family doctor, the doctor asked him a few questions, such as his full name, his birth date, his address, and asked him to repeat several seven-digit numbers. When he was unable to repeat the numbers accurately the doctor diagnosed him as having a mild case of dementia and told the woman that it was not uncommon for older people to develop this condition.

When their daily routine became anxiety-ridden with a number of incidents—such as his putting things away in unusual places and then accusing his wife of hiding them when he could not find them—in desperation she looked in the government section of the telephone directory and found a geriatric project director listed. This woman was a doctor associated with a mental health clinic who had 10% of her salary paid by a federal grant for geriatrics research. This doctor was one of the pioneers in Hawaii in the study and care of Alzheimer's patients, and after listening carefully to the wife she was able to assist her in developing a network of professionals in the health care field to provide support.

First the husband was given a thorough physical examination by an internist to rule out any thyroid problems or problems caused by medication that could contribute to dementia. This was followed by an EKG and CAT scan to rule out the possibilities of strokes or brain tumors. Finally, a neurologist diagnosed him as a patient with Alzheimer's disease.

Following this diagnosis the project director arranged for the wife and husband to call a family conference, and at this time their daughter, an only child, flew in from Connecticut. Through the project director, the family was introduced to the head of a geriatric education center, which was connected with a medical complex that housed an adult day-care center. Here they were assigned a social worker who would coordinate health care services for them. They were also introduced to an Alzheimer's disease support group that met on the Windward side, where the parents' apartment was located.

While a neighbor at their apartment complex remained with the father, the daughter and her mother attended a support group meeting. A representative of the state Alzheimer's association opened the meeting and asked for introductions. There were a half-dozen families represented that Saturday afternoon. There was a woman whose married daughters were visiting from Texas and Arizona to give her support because their father's condition was deteriorating, and the adult day-care facility was asking the family to seek other options.

A policeman was there to seek advice about his mother, who was diagnosed as having Alzheimer's disease but still insisted on living alone. He was accompanied by a colleague, a younger policeman who had seen his parents take care of his stricken grandmother for several years until her death. "A situation like this brings out the family dynamics," he explained. "My aunts and uncles never offered any help, and that really hurt the family relationship." He went on to explain that this brought the immediate family closer together as he and his siblings rallied around their parents to give them support. "Several weekends we children would send our parents on a trip to another island while we took over Grandmother's care," he said. "This experience brought out the best in us and helped us to appreciate our parents even more. One thing's for sure, if our parents ever become incapacitated, we're going to look after them the way they took care of Grandma."

In the island fashion the group welcomed the three mainland visitors and offered support. The group coordinator offered to facilitate health care services for the parents through the social workers, and several members offered to visit their parents and keep in touch by telephone.

The three women also mentioned that their parents' doctors were responsive and answered their questions to their satisfaction face-to-face as well as by long-distance telephone. One of the group members had just returned from a visit to the national headquarters of the Alzheimer's Disease and Related Disorders Association and informed them of its successful national campaigns and lobbying, resulting in its receiving $45 million for research and dissemination of information.

Hawaii, along with the other states, observes National Alzheimer's Week every fall. The state association, located in a shopping mall facing Ala Moana Park, has organized a network of dedicated support groups, consisting of people who have family members or friends with Alzheimer's disease. At their monthly meetings, the association has national and local professionals focus on topics from communication with Alzheimer's patients to the documentation of the living will. Professionals who attend the monthly meetings as speakers as well as participants include doctors, nurses, social workers, educators, care-home operators, counselors, lawyers, ministers, and psychologists and represent Hawaii's diverse ethnic groups. Support groups focus on specific problems and actively seek input from each family and interact with them. Support groups include caregivers and advocates of persons with Alzheimer's disease.

As the three daughters returned to their homes in Connecticut, Texas, and Arizona, they were able to offer support to their parents by telephone and by mail, in the context of a network of health care providers and friends. The daughters developed a multicultural "rainbow network" of supportive relationships in a state thousands of miles away.

Communication researchers have already found that interpersonal relationships can be enhanced through the telephone by appropriate nonverbal messages—paralanguage. Nonverbal vocal components of the speakers—such as pitch, loudness, and conversational speed—and voice quality affect the feelings and attitudes of the listeners. Multicultural training programs for distance communication address this need to develop the relational aspect of telecommunications (Kunimoto, 1981).

◆ Developing Multicultural
Communication Proficiency

In health care systems the relational context may have many combinations with many different outcomes. At a facility alone there are a number of provider-consumer relational combinations that can affect outcomes: doctor-patient, nurse-patient, medical technician-patient, clerk-patient, and attendant-patient. These different relational combinations are multiplied by the many different relationships established between the facility staff members in interprofessional, superordinate-subordinate, or peer combinations. Away from the health care facility there are other combinations of relational contexts for both patients and professionals. The impact that these relationships can have in health care settings is considerable.

Intercultural communication calls for relationship development that is sufficient to bridge intercultural gaps and to produce desired results—effective management, friendship, technology dissemination, conflict resolution, and training. Health care professionals provide a multitude of services from surgery to psychotherapy, services that call for proficiency in multicultural communication.

However, this proficiency does not exist merely because there are similarities of cultural background between professional and client. In some cases this similarity may lead to assumptions by one about the other that are inaccurate. The task of participants in the health care system, then, is to pay attention to the particular messages sent by others to understand what they are saying, rather than to stereotype them based on their cultural backgrounds (Wohl, 1989).

◆ Empowerment and Uncertainty Reduction

Empowerment is a buzzword that has pervaded the business sector as well as the health care setting. Management training for corporations has incorporated empowerment of employees as a way of increasing productivity. Empowerment—meaning "to enable," "to endow," "to invest," "to delegate," "to authorize," "to sanction"—was a key objective of the Americans With Disabilities Act, signed into law in 1990 and still being implemented throughout the United States. This act provides civil rights protections for all people with disabilities. It prohibits discrimination in hiring and requires accessibility to public accommodations and services. The implementation of this act is supposed to provide equal opportunities to all individuals with disabilities to participate in society to their greatest potential. This act is considered a form of social empowerment because it is designed to eliminate barriers that limit the activities and opportunities available to the physically and mentally disabled.

Unfortunately, the implementation of this act has focused on the introduction of ramps and elevators and other physical changes in organizational environments to provide physical access to the disabled but has not really adequately addressed the powerful cultural barriers of prejudice and stigma that have historically limited the opportunities available to the disabled in society (Kreps, 1993b). The Americans With Disabilities Act should have wide-ranging influence on health care delivery organizations because these organizations regularly serve the physically and mentally disabled, but to be really effective at empowering the disabled within health care contexts the act must promote enhanced cultural sensitivity, increased understanding and empathy, and the development of meaningful multicultural relations between the disabled and other participants in the modern health care system.

It is appropriate to reiterate the suggestion (Wohl, 1989) that *the task of the professional is to understand what the patient is saying as well as understand the patient's cultural differences.* To understand calls for listening, and Peters (1987), who has lectured to health care administrators as well as business executives, emphasizes that *empowering involves engaged listening* by the superordinate in the relationship. Engaged listening is a critical representation of concern that one person can communicate to others in any setting, but particularly in health care settings (Peters, 1987). Empowering a person means that you take that person seriously, and you demonstrate this by the action you take based on what you hear. Listening and acting on the information from the process reduces uncertainty, a primary barrier to effectiveness in multicultural communication.

Underpromising and overdelivering is another suggestion that Peters (1987) gives health care professionals and business executives alike. Some intriguing evidence from the health care field bears on this issue. Surgical patients who are told, in detail, of the nature of the post-operative agony recover as much as one-third faster than those left in the dark (Peters, 1987). Providing patients with full and accurate information, in language they can understand, about what they can expect from health care treatment, and allowing them to make knowledgeable choices about treatment is a moral and legal requirement of health care practice known as *informed consent.* Unfortunately, informed consent is not always communicated very well in health care practice and patients often make treatment decisions based on limited information (Kreps & Thornton, 1992; Waitzkin & Stoekle, 1972). Failure to provide patients with full treatment information inevitably leads to surprises that can be discomforting to patients. In contrast, providing full and accurate information helps consumers prepare for treatment and its repercussions.

Suppose a patient is told that he or she will suffer severe shortness of breath for four or five days following surgery. Even if the symptoms persist a bit longer than average, the patient is prepared to deal with it. The uninformed patient panics, believing that the operation was a failure. No amount of post-operative explanation helps ("They are lying—I'm dying"). Even if the uninformed patient's shortness of breath lasts less than the norm, his or her emotional distress frequently sets back overall recovery.

We all seek predictability. In fact, the more uncertain, frightening, and complex the situation, often amplified by the media, the more we grasp for predictability. That's why these health care findings are not at all surprising. And yet, as much as we may relate to such stories of frustrating, unkept promises, when we are on the receiving end (patient, consumer, commercial purchaser), we tend to underrate this concern when we plan our own firm's strategy.

We have seen the case of the Japanese-American executive who overcame cancer whose relationship with his oncologist was one of mutual respect and empowerment. The oncologist provided the executive with information on his illness, his prognosis, and protocols. Although the executive's physical appearance was Japanese, his physician did not rely on ethnic stereotypes to communicate interpersonally. He listened to his patient and considered his input in the decision-making process.

Even when the cancer recurred and the oncologist and his patient agreed that perhaps he was undertreated, there were no recriminations or harsh judgments. They were able to consider another experimental treatment, which turned out to be successful. Consider the differences in communication in our earlier example of the Japanese woman who was treated by a physician in Japan for cancer but who, however, was not informed of her disease. She was given no opportunity to consider options that may have saved her life.

All relationships are embedded within a larger social framework created by each dyad partner's separate communication networks and commitments. Knowing the foregoing can reduce uncertainty.

Several strategies are cited to reduce uncertainty in multicultural relationships (Infante, 1988): (1) passive—unobtrusive observation; (2) active—no direct contact, asking third parties; and (3) interactive—obtaining information directly. Professionals in health care settings generally use all three strategies.

During consultations in the office or during visits to the ward, health care providers interact with their patients, obtaining information directly and often recording the data. Nonverbal behavior of the patient and his or her family can be observed unobtrusively. In fact, the nonverbal messages observed during interactions—such as body language, paralanguage, and interactional distance—can provide important cues to the professional.

The active strategy of asking third parties to provide input is often used when patients (or others in the health care system) have difficulty articulating their concerns because of language problems, dementia, or apprehension. In the case of persons with Alzheimer's disease and other debilitating diseases, professionals often communicate with the patients' advocates or caregivers.

◆ Multicultural Dyads

The dyad is the building block of multicultural communication. We have mentioned previously that proficiency in multicultural communication may be developed by communication training. People who will be living or working in a culture different from their own often undergo culture-specific training. Professionals who work in multicultural health care settings often undergo culture-general training. Culture training focuses on sensitizing individuals to rules and norms of their own culture and indicating general categories of cross-cultural differences, such as differences in verbal and nonverbal codes. Culture-general training makes people more receptive and sensitive to cultural differences by making them more aware of the biases and limitations their own culture imposes on them. Such training would help them to become more flexible in inferring motives or attributing meaning to another's behavior, thus increasing their proficiency in multicultural communication. Such persons would become more aware of the possibilities of different interpretations of communication (Bastien, 1987).

Researchers who have analyzed a number of methods of developing multicultural communication proficiency have suggested that practitioners develop a theory-oriented mind-set and people skills (Dodd, 1991; Koester, Wiseman, & Sanders, 1993; Martin, 1993). Theories, such as uncertainty reduction, are useful for understanding past performance, interpreting current behaviors, and predicting future actions (Griffin, 1991; Gudykunst, 1988). People skills, proficiency in developing multicultural relationships, is a key to one's productivity as a physician or nurse, supervisor or clerk, social worker or ambulance driver, caregiver or patient (Bolton, 1986).

Multicultural communication proficiency is affected ultimately by the two essential notions of content and relationship. Our relationship with the person with whom we are communicating affects how the message is interpreted. Conversely, messages also alter relationships (Watzlawick, Beavin & Jackson, 1967). *Bandura's (1986) social cognitive theory* and *concept of modeling* amplifies the integration of content and relationship. To enhance the building block of multicultural communication—the dyad—one must develop a personal style of interpersonal communication that strengthens the relationship and is mutually empowering. This reinforces a focus that includes information gain, attitude change or reinforcement, and skill acquisition as objectives of a training program to develop multicultural communication proficiency.

4

Communicating in Multicultural Groups in Health Care

They empower us
Energize and harmonize
Groups both large and small.

◆ The Role of the Group in Health Care

The small group is an important and ubiquitous work unit and social collective in health care (Cline, 1990). Consumers and providers organize into small groups to accomplish complex tasks and make important decisions (Kreps & Thornton, 1992). Health care groups can be formal, organizationally based units—such as operating room teams, health care delivery teams, multidisciplinary consultation groups, review boards, and ethics committees—or they can be informal groups of peers, friends, coworkers, and family members that provide group members with social support and relevant health information.

Both formal and informal groups dramatically influence health care (Kreps, 1990a). Clearly, formal groups that perform specific health care activities, such as health care teams that coordinate the activities of members in the provision of health care services, have significant influences on health care (see Thornton, 1978; Thornton, McCoy, & Baldwin, 1980).

Informal groups, such as the family unit and peer support groups, are also likely to exert great influence on health care. Because the family is the primary setting for cultural socialization, in which each individual's culturally held beliefs about health and health care are developed, the family is a group that has enormous influences on individual health behaviors (Becker, 1974; Gochman, 1972). Many of the beliefs you have about health and health care that influence the kinds of behaviors you engage in probably originated from your experiences interacting within your family.

Group members are able to achieve far more collectively, through coordination of activities, than they could individually. That is why groups are used so often in health care to address complex issues and long-range problems. The systems theory concept of *nonsummativity* suggests that in a well-organized system, such as a small group, the whole is more than the sum of its parts. This is due to the synergistic effect of cooperation. *Synergy* is the extra energy generated by cooperation. Therefore, the most effective groups are those that are well coordinated and cooperative. As we examine in this chapter, effective multicultural relations are essential to developing cooperative, coordinated, and synergistic health care groups.

◆ Communication and Group Performance

Communication performs a major role in eliciting cooperation and coordination among group members. Because individual group members have their own personal goals and behavioral agendas, they are probably not predisposed to give up their own plans and follow the directions of other group members. Each member must be persuaded to adapt his or her personal agenda to the group agenda, coordinating activities with others to enable groups to be synergistic. Such cooperation can be elicited through communication, through messages that convey relevant and persuasive information, providing group members with rationale and direction for coordinating activities (Kreps, 1988a; 1990a).

Sometimes in groups cooperation is requested overtly, such as when group members make specific requests of one another. ("You do this and you do that.") Often, cooperation is elicited subtly, over time, as group members interact and get to know what each other expects of them, responding to information conveyed verbally and nonverbally. Based on such communication, group members often agree to coordinate activities and share responsibility for achieving group goals. These agreements to cooperate are important building blocks for effective group process, especially in health care groups, in which cooperation and coordination are essential.

In effective health care groups, members develop cooperative interpersonal relationships, based on the mutual agreements they have established to follow each other's directives. These agreements are often referred to as *implicit contracts*, where, through the course of interpersonal communication, relational partners learn about specific expectations each holds and are motivated to meet these expectations (Kreps, 1990a; Kreps & Thornton, 1992; Rossiter & Pearce, 1975). For example, implicit contracts are likely to be established among members of a health care review board assigned to evaluate the performance of a specific health care system. The implicit contracts that have been established guide board members' interdependent data-gathering activities so each member is directed to probe different aspects of the system's performance, sharing the information gathered and maximizing the group's ability to effectively evaluate the health care system. Similarly, members of a surgical team might establish implicit contracts that guide each member to perform different tasks during an operation, such as providing surgeons with the correct surgical tools, suctioning blood from the incision when necessary, and keeping track of equipment readouts monitoring physical condition to provide relevant feedback about the patient's vital signs. The ability of these team members to establish clear and motivating implicit contracts for coordinating these activities is of utmost importance and is likely to have a strong influence on the success of the operation.

In addition to using communication to coordinate activities, group members use communication to provide one another with relevant information for accomplishing group goals. Each group member brings a different perspective to the issues facing health care groups, based on his or her unique cultural orientations, professional training, and personal experiences. These unique perspectives are of great value to group performance, enabling group members to compare a range of ideas concerning a given issue and identify different strategic courses of action.

By sharing relevant information about an issue facing the group, members help their groups accomplish both task and socioemotional goals (Benne & Sheats, 1948; Kreps & Thornton, 1992). *Task goals* involve accomplishment of the formally designated job activities and functions of a group. Group members also help accomplish *socioemotional goals* by maintaining the social equilibrium of the group. Socioemotional communication can achieve these goals by showing support, relieving pressure, and being attentive, when appropriate, to help group members work together harmoniously (Kreps & Thornton, 1992).

◆ Culture and Group Process

Culture plays an important role in health care groups. The unique composition and cultural backgrounds of members within health care groups are key group variables in group process. Cultural variables—such as members' professional background, organizational position, age, or gender—can dramatically influence group performance. Culture influences the kinds of expectations and interpretations members are likely to have of group activities and strategies.

Members of health care groups are likely to possess quite distinct culturally based perspectives on the activities and issues facing the group. These unique cultural perspectives can be likened to a double-edged sword that can both help and hurt group process. On the negative side of this sword, unique cultural perspectives can be major impediments to agreement within the group, leading to impasses in group progress. However, on the positive side of this double-edged sword, these unique perspectives can also provide the group with excellent insights and directions for accomplishing goals. For example, in a health care team, members are likely to represent different health care professions (such as different branches of medicine, nursing, physical and occupational therapy, pharmacy, or social work), and as such will inevitably have differences in their professional training, perspectives on how to treat particular health problems, and experiences with the health care issues handled by the team. These cultural differences can be a barrier to group progress, leading to mistrust and resentment, if team members are unable to use communication to work out differences in opinion and negotiate group decisions. With effective multicultural communication these different points of view are likely to provide the team with a range of ideas that shed insights into complex issues and identify alternative courses of group action. Thus, the quality of multicultural relations among team members in health care can dramatically influence the effectiveness of these groups.

The cultural identities of group members are among the most important initial conditions influencing health care groups, because culture strongly influences member beliefs and behaviors. Group members must interact with each other in ways that will encourage all members to apply their unique cultural perspectives (valuable expertise and insights) to the accomplishment of group goals, by sharing relevant information, generating new ideas and solutions to problems, providing social support, and engendering cooperation.

From a systems theoretical perspective, culture can be seen as an important input variable influencing groups. For example, the cultural differences and similarities (group inputs) between individual members of health care teams inevitably influence team activities (group process) and outcomes (group output).

INPUT —————————————→ PROCESS ————————————→ OUTPUT

Figure 4.1. The Systems Transformation Model

Groups are social systems that process information to accomplish goals (Berrien, 1968, 1976; Weick, 1979).

The *systems transformation model* (see Figure 4.1) describes how the initial starting conditions (inputs) in groups—such as personnel, resources, or equipment—are coordinated and transformed by group members (process) to achieve desired individual and group goals (outputs). This model illustrates that to accomplish formal goals, groups must be able to effectively transform initial *inputs* (such as the cultural orientations and expertise of group members) into advantageous *outputs* (group actions, decisions, and policies). Multicultural communication is an important social process that enables effective health care groups to engender cooperation in synergistically transforming their initial inputs into desired group outputs.

◆ Multicultural Relations and Health Care Teams

Health care teams are important work units in modern health care systems. Teams are groups of people involved in the delivery of health care, often representing different health care disciplines and perspectives, who work together to collaboratively provide health care services (Kreps & Thornton, 1992). By working in teams health care providers and consumers are able to share relevant health information and coordinate the delivery of health care services. The effectiveness of health care teams, however, depends on the quality of communication among team members (Thornton, 1978; Thornton, McCoy, & Baldwin, 1980; Wise, 1974).

Consumers of health care should be recognized as a central part of any health care team, although unfortunately in actual

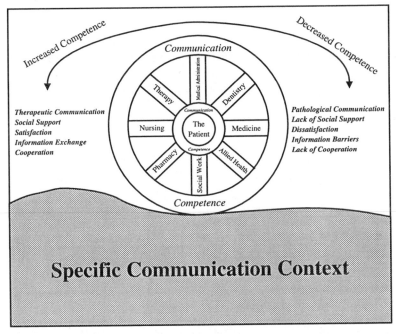

Figure 4.2. Model of Relational Health Communication Competence

SOURCE: Reprinted from Gary L. Kreps (1988), Relational communication in health care, *Southern Communication Journal, 53*, 344-359.

practice clients are not always included as team members or allowed to participate in team meetings and discussions. Interestingly, research has shown that consumer involvement in health care decision making improves physical response to treatment (Greenfield, Kaplan, & Ware, 1985; Roter, 1983). Therefore, clients should be encouraged to participate actively in making decisions concerning their care.

Notice in *Kreps's (1988a) model of relational health communication competence* (see Figure 4.2) how the consumer (patient) is at the center of the health care wheel (team), depicted as the axle of the wheel. The different health care providers are illustrated as the different spokes of the wheel that surround the patient. Lines of communication connect the health care providers to one another and to the consumer. The more competent the communication is between these members of the health care team, the more likely the team is to promote therapeutic communication, social support, satisfaction, information exchange, and cooperation. The less competent the communication is among team members, the more likely the team is to promote pathological communication, lack of social support, dissatisfaction, information barriers, and lack of cooperation.

The tendency to exclude clients from membership in health care teams may be due to unresolved intercultural barriers between providers and consumers. Such exclusion of clients can reflect providers' lack of respect for the important role consumers can perform in team activities. Because of *stereotyping* and *ethnocentrism* (recall our discussion of these processes in Chapter 1), health care providers may underestimate the level of health care knowledge consumers possess, assuming that consumers are unlikely to be able to comprehend the health care issues examined within the team and are therefore unprepared to participate effectively in team meetings (Pratt, Seligmann, & Reader, 1957; Seligmann, McGrath, & Pratt, 1957).

Providers may also fail to recognize the importance of consumers' personal experiences in diagnosing, selecting, and evaluating treatment strategies, thus underestimating the benefits of collaborating with clients in teams when making treatment decisions (Kreps & Thornton, 1992; Roter, 1983) Since the primary focus of health care services is to serve the consumer, providers can use the opportunity to interact with clients within health care teams to learn more about the needs and experiences of these consumers. The information gathered in team discussions can be used to guide health care treatment strategies.

As we mentioned in Chapter 3 regarding *informed consent*, consumers have the right to obtain (and health care practitioners have the obligation to provide) full and clear information about recommended health care procedures and their potential effects so clients can make knowledgeable decisions about accepting or rejecting such treatment (Ingelfinger, 1972). Consumers can learn more about health care treatment strategies though active participation in health care teams, and providers can help consumers with access to the relevant health information necessary to enable them to make well-informed choices about treatment.

Health care consumers may not be assertive enough to claim their right to informed consent or to participate actively in health care teams. When confused, consumers are often embarrassed to ask health care providers for clarification. When asked whether they understand complex explanations and instructions, they may sheepishly nod their heads yes rather than admit their confusion. Health care providers must be receptive and responsive to the information and communication needs of consumers, inviting consumers to participate fully in health care decision making. Consumer participation in health care teams can help promote increased cooperation and collaboration between providers and consumers.

Poor *interprofessional relations* among health care providers can be a major impediment to effective health care delivery (Boyer, Lee, & Kirschner, 1977; Frank, 1961; Hill, 1978; Kindig, 1975). Team members representing different health care professions (medicine, nursing, pharmacy, social work, etc.) are often *ethnocentric* about the superiority of their own professional perspectives on health care, believing their individual orientations are the only legitimate ones, and are resistant to accepting the perspectives of other team members (Kreps & Thornton, 1992). Even representatives of the different branches of medicine (surgery, internal medicine, psychiatry, etc.) have been known to stereotype one another, with surgeons feeling superior to internists and pediatricians feeling superior to psychiatrists (Friedson, 1970). These cultural biases can significantly limit cooperation and synergy in health care teams.

Health care providers are socialized through their educational and work experiences to develop strong professional identities. These professional identities are strong cultural influences on member beliefs, attitudes, and values. Communication across different professional groups can often become strained because of cultural barriers (Frank, 1961; Hill, 1978). Kreps and Thornton (1992) explain that culturally based constraints that can separate health care professionals and often erode cooperation between health care providers may include differences in educational backgrounds, career patterns, language use, socioeconomic status, gender, race, values, and lack of interprofessional familiarity and respect. These interprofessional cultural biases must be minimized for health care teams to be effective.

The most effective health care teams are *egalitarian* groups, in which all members are treated as equals (Kreps & Thornton, 1984; Thornton, 1978; Thornton, McCoy, & Baldwin, 1980). Evidence suggests that physicians often attempt to dominate health care teams, undermining the development of egalitarianism (Friedson, 1970; Yanda, 1977). To develop egalitarian teams, the cultural barriers that separate group members must be removed and interprofessional respect and acceptance must be promoted.

A first step in promoting egalitarianism in health care teams is to educate team members about the specialized expertise and contribution each team member, including the client, can offer to the team (Boyer, Lee, & Kirschner, 1977; Kindig, 1975; Wise, 1974). When teams are first formed, members should go through team-building and orientation training sessions. In these sessions the importance of cooperation between team members, the need for balancing task and socioemotional roles, and the development of interprofessional respect should be stressed. Each health care practitioner can provide an overview of his or her area of expertise during these training sessions to acquaint other team members with the kinds of contributions each person can make to team deliberations. Rather than having fixed leadership within the team, leadership can be alternated so the member with the greatest specialized knowledge on an issue under consideration can direct group deliberations. Developing interprofessional respect, coordination, and egalitarianism can help the health care team fully utilize group member expertise and work together to effectively deliver care (Gifford, 1983).

◆ Ethics Committees

Ethics committees are review groups that provide counsel in health care systems about making complex decisions concerning moral and bioethical issues involved in health research and health care. These committees are generally composed of an interdisciplinary group of health care providers, administrators, social workers, chaplains, patient representatives, lawyers, and at times selected members of the relevant public (Bosford, 1986; Thornton, 1993). Ethics committees may help a hospital evaluate the moral issues involved in making decisions about many different situations, such as when to provide treatment to or withhold it from a terminally ill patient, when to use or discontinue use of placebo drugs with clinical trial research subjects who are seriously ill and are likely to benefit from established medications, or which patient among many seriously ill applicants on a waiting list for a heart transplant should receive the next available donated organ. These are very difficult decisions to make and there are many relevant issues to consider in rendering ethical decisions; yet, modern health care systems are faced with these tough decisions every day. Ethics committees carefully deliberate the issues concerning these cases and examine available options and the implications of different courses of action for all parties concerned, ultimately providing health care administrators with evaluations of the issues to guide decision making and to set policies for guiding future actions.

The earliest ethics committees developed in response to the moral dilemma facing health care delivery organizations during the 1960s and early 1970s in selecting candidates for hemodialysis treatment, prior to the federal government's ruling in 1972 to fund all treatment for end-stage renal disease (Ross, Bayley, Michel, & Pugh, 1986). Ethics committees were used to help make life-or-death decisions about which kidney disease patients to select out of a large pool of worthy candidates. The ethics committees helped hospitals justify to the public (and to those hemodialysis candidates that were not selected for treatment) that all candidates were fairly evaluated and an equitable process was used to select those for treatment. Other early ethics committees were used to help health care systems make difficult decisions about *euthanasia*, such as in the well-publicized case of Karen Ann Quinlan, in which the New Jersey Supreme Court in 1972 recommended that an ethics committee be consulted in determining whether to withhold medical treatment (Ross, Bayley, Michel, & Pugh, 1986; Thornton, 1993).

Culture directly influences ethical standards and behaviors. Ethical values are established by cultures, and determinations about ethical courses of action must take relevant cultural orientations into account. "Through the acculturation and socialization processes we are trained to recognize ethical constraints on our behavior. Right and wrong are intimately tied to the cultural groups to which we belong. Ethics play a major role in the health care delivery system, and the different cultural orientations of health professionals and consumers of health care instigate a situation where a wide range of moral and ethical positions are often in competition with one another" (Kreps & Thornton, 1984, pp. 201-202).

Culture is a key topic of examination for ethics committees. There are societal standards for behavior (often enforced through legal mandates), religious standards, and professional standards that must be considered in making *bioethical decisions*. For example, euthanasia is an issue that is receiving a great deal of current attention in the United States. Jack Kevorkian, MD, a physician from the state of Michigan, has received national attention for his efforts to assist terminally ill individuals in committing suicide. In an attempt to curtail the euthanasia activities of Kevorkian, the state of Michigan has established new laws to prevent assisted suicides. Different religious groups, health care agencies, and citizens' groups have alternately supported and condemned Kevorkian's actions. These different reactions to euthanasia reflect different cultural values and orientations. In evaluating Kevorkian's use of euthanasia, an ethics committee would have to take into consideration all of these different cultural perspectives, especially the cultural orientation of the terminally ill individuals who seek his help in committing suicide, to identify ethical courses of action.

Because ethics committees are comprised of interdisciplinary and interprofessional sets of members, these groups are likely to possess a broad range of cultural perspectives that enables them to examine diverse cultural orientations on ethical issues. However, committee interaction must demonstrate respect for these different cultural perspectives and encourage group members to actively share their cultural experiences in the group evaluations of ethical issues. Effective multicultural relations among the members of ethics committees is essential to enabling these groups to engage in effective deliberation of bioethical issues.

Moreover, ethics committees must often seek relevant information from sources external to the committee, taking into account the relevant cultural perspectives of all individuals involved in the issues under examination, to fully evaluate bioethical decisions and courses of action. Effective multicultural relations, then, are essential not only within the committee but also between ethics committee members and relevant publics from whom they must gather pertinent cultural information.

◆ Social Support Groups

Social support is a communicative process that helps troubled individuals work through the anxiety and uncertainty of difficult and stressful life events (Albrecht & Adelman, 1987; Kreps & Thornton, 1992). Social support is provided informally in everyday life by friends and family members, as well as formally by counselors and *self-help groups*. Although the family is the principal informal group setting for social support (Dean & Lin, 1977), in recent years many self-help groups have emerged as important formal settings for the provision of social support, helping individuals cope with such diverse issues as bereavement (Cluck & Cline, 1986), divorce (Chiraboga, Coho,

Stein, & Roberts, 1979), epilepsy (Arntson & Droge, 1987), cancer (Heiney & Wells, 1989; Peters-Golden, 1982), HIV/AIDS (Ribble, 1989), hospice work (Richman, 1989), old age (Campbell & Chenoweth, 1981; Query, 1985), and mental illness (Horowitz, 1977).

Social support groups help their members cope with life stress through communication, by providing them with relevant information about "health care methods and services, problem solving interaction, referral services, friendly visits, and assistance in making choices about health care options available to them. These groups help members feel good about themselves and assert control of their own health care" (Kreps, 1988b, p. 249). Social support groups use communication to *empower* their members.

Individuals join support groups because the normative ways for coping with life stresses learned through cultural socialization are no longer working for them. They need to develop new cultural norms for addressing these problems. Support group interaction helps members establish new cultural norms for handling difficult life experiences, providing members with new cultural frameworks for viewing the world and responding to it. For example, one of the oldest and best known self-help groups, Alcoholics Anonymous, provides its members with a very strong cultural framework that guides member behaviors. This cultural framework evolves out of group rituals and rules that socialize members into the group's culture. Primary group rituals and rules include identification of members as recovering alcoholics, the expectation that members will attend meetings where they will give public testimony to their personal responsibility for causing their drinking problems, and the expectation that members will provide support to other members to help them refrain from drinking alcohol (Northouse & Northouse, 1992). The strength of this self-help group's cultural socialization process has made it a very influential social support group and one of the most successful long-term treatments for alcoholism.

Cultural sensitivity is an important element of effective support groups. Cline (1990) describes several aspects of cultural sensitivity when she suggests that "the effectiveness of self-help groups appears to be dependent on nurturing a highly cohesive group whose goals are attainable only through communication characterized by reciprocal self-disclosure, empathic honesty, acceptance, and symmetrical interaction" (p. 78). Members of peer support groups often share similar cultural experiences that promote mutual acceptance and identification, facilitating their development of cohesive and nurturing groups.

Members are particularly vulnerable when they enter support groups. Their confidence is often shaken; they are confused and they are need help in coping with their problems. Culturally sensitive communication can help support-group members reduce uncertainty, regain their confidence, and identify new strategies for handling their problems (Kreps & Thornton, 1992).

◆ Conclusion

Groups can perform important functions in health care if group members work together cooperatively and synergistically. Member cooperation depends on the development of intercultural respect, so group members feel comfortable enough to develop meaningful implicit contracts for guiding collaboration. In this chapter we have described the important health care functions performed by health care teams, ethics committees, and social support groups. Sensitive multicultural communication is essential to the effective operation of these health care groups.

| 5

Communicating in Multicultural Health Care Organizations

Organizations
Supportive networks reach out
To heal heart and soul.

◆ The Organization of Modern Health Care

Health care consumers are increasingly dependent on health care delivery organizations, such as hospitals, clinics, nursing homes, health maintenance organizations (HMOs), and group practices (Starr, 1982). These organizations, as the primary sites for formal health care delivery, are important subsystems within the modern *health care system*.

Modern health care delivery organizations are often large, complex, and *decentralized* (having many different departments and divisions, each with distinct missions, functions, and procedures), housing an interdependent mix of differentially trained health care professionals, support staff, and specialized technologies necessary to provide many different health care services to a wide range of consumers (Perrow, 1965; Starr, 1982). Unfortunately, the very complexity of these organizations that enables them to serve a broad range of consumers also makes these modern health care delivery systems increasingly *bureaucratic* (having many rules and procedures), intimidating, and confusing for many consumers (as well as for providers), significantly limiting the effectiveness of modern health care delivery (Illich, 1976; Kreps, 1990a, 1990b; Mendelsohn, 1979).

The multicultural mix of health care providers and consumers that populates modern health care delivery organizations adds to the complexity of these systems. As we discuss in this chapter, a major challenge in modern health care is to promote effective multicultural relations among the many different interdependent staff members, providers, and consumers that comprise modern health care delivery organizations.

To accomplish the related goals of health promotion and preservation, health care organizations depend on cooperation and coordination between interdependent health care providers, health care administrators, staff members, and consumers to effectively provide health care services (Kreps, 1988b). Communication is the essential social process in these health care systems for eliciting cooperation and coordination among interdependent health care providers, consumers and administrators (Costello & Pettegrew, 1979; Kreps & Thornton, 1992; Ray & Miller, 1990). Yet, the communication competencies needed by participants in the modern health care system to elicit necessary coordination for effectively accomplishing health care goals are often very elusive in actual health care practice (Kreps & Query, 1989; Kreps & Thornton, 1992).

◆ Communication and Multicultural Relations

It is not easy to elicit cooperation between interdependent members of health care systems because of culturally based differences in individual backgrounds, orientations, strategies, and goals. For example, health care providers and consumers, because of their different educational backgrounds and personal orientations, are likely to perceive the same health care situations quite differently and have different expectations for treatment and health outcomes. It is a significant challenge for health care providers and consumers to communicate multiculturally in ways that will promote the sharing of culturally based health beliefs and expectations, enabling these interdependent participants in the modern health care system to clearly understand each other, ameliorate differences in opinion, and mutually influence each other's behaviors in coordinating health care delivery (Ballard-Reisch, 1990, 1993; Kreps & Thornton, 1992).

The complexity and importance of sharing relevant culturally based health information in the modern health care system cannot be emphasized strongly enough. For example, health care providers and their clients depend on sharing relevant health information to jointly make important diagnostic and treatment decisions. Yet, because of cultural differences in power, status, and expertise between health care providers and consumers, it is not uncommon for patients to defer to their physicians' judgments about the nature of their ailments and the best way to treat these problems rather than to participate actively in jointly making decisions about their own health care (Ballard-Reisch, 1990, 1993; Greenfield, Kaplan, & Ware, 1985; O'Hair, 1986). Because of status differences, patients are often reticent about sharing relevant information concerning their health conditions and experiences with health care providers (Kreps & Thornton, 1992). Furthermore, providers often fail to encourage full patient disclosure and participation, preferring to communicate *to* patients rather than *with* patients (Burgoon, Parrott, Burgoon, Birk, Pfau, & Coker, 1987; Greenfield, Kaplan, & Ware, 1985; O'Hair, O'Hair, Southward, & Krayer, 1987; Waitzkin & Stoekle, 1976). The bureaucracy of the modern health care system exacerbates this communication problem by reinforcing status differences and distance between providers and consumers. In this chapter we examine how communication in modern health care delivery organizations can be used to minimize cultural distance between providers and consumers to promote the sharing of relevant cultural information in health care.

Not only is there too much cultural distance between consumers and providers in modern health care, there are often cultural barriers to effective communication among the many specialists, administrators, and other health care professionals who must work together cooperatively in health care delivery organizations. It is often a significant challenge for interdependent health care providers to communicate effectively with one another (establish effective *interprofessional relations*), especially when these individuals are members of different (and often competing) *professional cultures* (Kreps & Thornton, 1992).

Health care providers from different professional cultures usually have gone through different educational and training programs, have different job titles, belong to different professional organizations, and have different health care duties and experiences. Because of differences in their professional training (such as the different educational emphases experienced by surgeons, psychologists, nutritionists, pathologists, pharmacists, internists, and registered nurses) and distinct professional orientations towards health care, different providers are likely to make different decisions about which health care intervention strategies are best for treating a particular consumer's health problems. These differences of clinical judgment are important issues to consider when developing an effective multidisciplinary *holistic treatment* (treating the whole person and not just one aspect, such as the pulmonary or respiratory systems, of the person) regimen.

There is very likely to be merit to each of the clinical approaches advocated by the different providers, and a combination of treatment strategies is likely to be warranted. However, without effective multicultural interaction between these interdependent health care providers it is unlikely they will be receptive to sharing and using such relevant treatment information in collaboratively developing the best strategies for patient care. In fact, it is not uncommon for one of these health care providers (usually the one with the highest professional status within the health care system) to ethnocentrically dictate health care treatment decisions without actively consulting other professionals, and in doing so limit the exchange of relevant diagnostic and clinical health information and minimize the potential for effective holistic health care treatment (Freidson, 1975).

Effective multicultural relations can help to reduce many of the complexities inherent in modern health care systems by facilitating the exchange of relevant health information, promoting enhanced interprofessional understanding and respect between interdependent members of the health care team (including consumers of health care), and eliciting cooperation and coordination in the delivery of health care services (Kavanaugh & Kennedy, 1992).

Conversely, ineffective multicultural relations in health care organizations inevitably exacerbate the complexity of modern health care by inhibiting the sharing of relevant information, decreasing interpersonal understanding, and alienating interdependent members of the health care system. In this chapter we examine many of the challenges to effective multicultural relations in modern organizations, identify several primary issues and settings for multicultural relations in modern health care, and suggest specific strategies for promoting effective multicultural communication in the health care system.

◆ The Role of Communication in Organizing

Human communication is the primary social process that enables human beings to organize (Kreps, 1990a). Individuals communicate to establish cooperative *interpersonal relationships* that are the building blocks of modern organizations. Through communication, organization members share relevant information about their expectations for and reactions to each other, developing relational agreements to coordinate their activities in the accomplishment of individual and organizational goals. For example, in health care delivery systems doctors must communicate effectively with their patients to establish cooperative provider-consumer relationships, gather relevant diagnostic information, and provide clear and persuasive directions for treatment.

Organizational communication is complex, because it encompasses each of the three levels of communication (*intrapersonal communication, interpersonal communication,* and *group communication*) discussed in the previous chapters in this book. Organizational communication also goes beyond the intrapersonal, interpersonal, and group levels of interaction to include *intergroup relations* (communication between representatives of different groups) and *interorganizational relations* (communication between representatives of different related organizations).

Communication is used to coordinate activities at these multiple organizational levels. It is used both internally to facilitate cooperation among members of the same organizations and externally to elicit cooperation among representatives of different organizations. Within the health care system, for example, communication is used to elicit cooperation among health care consumers and their providers, among members of health care teams, among representatives of different hospital departments, and even among an incredibly broad range of different health care delivery and support organizations (such as health care equipment and supply companies, insurance companies, food service companies, volunteer organizations, charitable organizations, relief organizations, public media organizations, consumer groups, accrediting boards, employment agencies, external consultants, and government agencies).

◆ Internal and External Organizational Communication

There are two primary interdependent channels of organizational communication: *internal channels of communication* and *external channels of communication* (Kreps, 1990a). Internal communication occurs among members of the same organization. It is referred to as *internal* communication because it occurs within the boundaries of a single organization. Internal communication is used to perform important administrative functions such as providing job instructions, directing task accomplishment, and providing performance evaluation.

External communication occurs among members of an organization and individuals who are not part of that organization, often with individuals who are representatives of groups within the organization's *relevant environment*. An organization's relevant environment is composed of all the individuals, groups, and organizations that influence and are influenced by the organization, including potential clients, suppliers, regulatory agencies, competing organizations, and media representatives. External communication is referred to as *external* because it involves the exchange of messages beyond the boundaries of the organization. External communication is used to establish good *public relations* with members of the relevant environment by *providing* these external publics with relevant information (such as annual reports, health education publications, press releases, or advertisements), by *gathering* information about external issues of relevance to the organization, and by *promoting* coordination between the organization and key members of its relevant environment.

Multicultural relations dramatically influence the quality of both internal and external communication in the modern health care system. Internal communication in health care involves coordinating the activities of an increasingly diverse population of organizational members. The full gamut of cultural diversity described in the first chapter of this book (differences based on nationality, ethnicity, age, gender, education, profession, socioeconomic status, health status, etc.) are evident in modern health care.

Interprofessional cooperation is a particularly critical issue in the provision of health care services. Yet, as we have discussed earlier, cultural barriers and ethnocentrism often inhibit cooperation among health care providers representing different specialties and professional groups. Cultural distance between the providers of health care and consumers of health care can limit the effectiveness of multicultural relations in health care, seriously impeding the exchange of relevant information and the development of cooperative provider-consumer relationships. Multicultural sensitivity must be promoted in health care organizations if internal channels of communication are to be effective.

Multicultural relations also influence the quality of external organizational communication in health care delivery organizations. Modern health care delivery organizations serve a very diverse public, including a broad range of different potential consumers, government agencies, regulatory groups, unions, medical supply companies, insurance companies, and benefactors. Health care organizations must tailor their external communication efforts to match the specific cultural perspectives of these different external audiences. No one generic message strategy is likely to satisfy the broad diversity of different publics that comprise the relevant environments of modern health care delivery organizations.

For external communication to be effective, representatives of health care organizations must first identify the relevant publics they need to communicate with, segment these publics into specific (relatively homogenous) audiences, gather relevant cultural information from each of these audiences to identify their culturally based information needs and orientations (*audience analysis*), and then develop culturally sensitive communication strategies for providing these groups with relevant health information, meeting these audiences' needs and expectations, and initiating cooperative external relationships. For example, hospitals often engage in external *communication campaigns* to raise funds, soliciting public financial support through individual and corporate donations. No one fund-raising message strategy will work equally well with all audiences. Different message strategies must be used to encourage different potential donors to support the organization. One potential donor may be most interested in the hospital's health risk prevention programs, another potential donor may be more concerned about the availability of the latest health care technologies in the hospital, and a third potential donor may be most interested in the moral values exhibited by the hospital. Successful fund-raising campaigns will employ specifically tailored culturally sensitive external messages for each of these potential donors that focus on the specific interests of each of these audiences to encourage their financial support of the hospital.

◆ Balancing Innovation and Stability in Health Care

Effective coordination of internal and external channels of organizational communication enables organizations to maintain an often precarious, yet critically important, *balance between innovation and stability* in organizational life (Kreps, 1990a). Both innovation and stability are important features of organizational life. Innovation is needed to enable organizations to change in response to inevitable constraints and opportunities that emerge over time. Stability is needed to provide structure and predictability.

In health care organizations, for example, internal channels of communication are generally used to prescribe specific job descriptions and provide training for health care professionals that facilitates coordination between interdependent providers. Similarly, external channels of communication are often used to provide hospital representatives with relevant information, perhaps about new federal regulations for health care, that enables the organization to innovate its activities to meet these new regulations.

Too much stability or innovation can threaten organizational survival. Too much innovation, for example, can make organizational life unpredictable and confusing for organization members, whereas too much stability can make it difficult for organizations to respond to changing conditions. The challenge of organizing is to effectively balance innovation and stability.

Kreps (1990a) describes the organizational communication strategy of *relative openness* to help organizations maintain a balance between stability and innovation. Relative openness matches organizational use of internal and external communication to the source (internal or external) and extent of *information turbulence*. Turbulence refers to situations in which individuals have difficulty making sense of organizational life, in which conditions are uncertain, equivocal, and volatile (Kreps, 1990a; Weick, 1979). Internal turbulence occurs when there are high levels of uncertainty and change within an organization, such as when a company declares bankruptcy and members are not sure whether the organization will survive or whether they will be able to keep their jobs. External turbulence occurs when there are high levels of uncertainty within the relevant environment, such as during natural environmental crises (floods or earthquakes) or during challenging social changes (periods of economic instability, changing government regulations, or even the introduction of powerful new technologies of relevance to the organization).

Relative openness suggests that in response to internal turbulence organizations should restrict communications with the relevant environment and focus attention on the use of internal channels of communication to gather information from organization members about the turbulence they are experiencing and to provide these organization members with relevant information to reduce their uncertainty. In times of external turbulence organizations should be relatively open to their environment, focusing attention on their use of external channels of communication to gather information from and provide relevant information to key external audiences.

Cultural diversity is often a significant challenge to organizational stability, because people who have different cultural orientations are likely to see the world in very different ways and to act in accord with different implicit cultural norms. Internal communication must be used in multicultural social systems, such as health care delivery organizations, to help make the divergent cultural norms and expectations of culturally diverse populations of organization members explicit, fostering understanding and respect for differences among members.

Internal communication can also be used to promote *cultural convergence* by establishing new organizationally based cultural norms for guiding coordination among organization members. (We examine further this issue of cultural convergence through the development of organizationally based cultural norms later in this chapter when we discuss organizational culture).

In effective health care organizations multicultural communication is used to help culturally diverse organization members develop strategies for cooperation and coordination to promote organizational stability, overcoming the inherent destabilizing tendencies of multiple cultural orientations. Similarly, external channels of organizational communication should be used to promote cooperation between health care organizations and their relevant environments, counteracting the natural culturally based tendencies diverse publics often have to act idiosyncratically. Organization members can enhance organizational stability by using internal and external channels of communication to promote cultural convergence, developing shared norms across diverse cultural groups inside and outside of the organization.

Although cultural diversity often works against the goal of achieving organizational stability, diversity often has the distinct benefit of enhancing organizational innovation by providing fresh ideas, new solutions to difficult problems, and innovative approaches to organizing. In our earlier discussion of the *theory of weak ties* (presented in the first chapter), we explained how people from different cultural backgrounds (weak ties) are likely to provide each other with many new ideas because each cultural group has been socialized to see and cope with the world in very different ways. The *strength of weak ties* is that cultural diversity provides organizations with different sources of relevant information and novel strategies for achieving important organizational goals. Health care delivery systems should use internal and external channels of organizational communication to demonstrate respect for and encourage the sharing of culturally diverse ideas and interpretations of organizational reality, encouraging the use of such multicultural interaction in creative problem solving and innovation generation in organizational life. For example, by establishing a diverse membership in health care teams, ethics committees, and other decision-making groups in health care organizations, these groups are likely to generate a broad range of innovative strategies for accomplishing organizational goals.

◆ Formal and Informal Organizational Communication

There are also formal and informal lines of organizational communication. *Formal organizational communication* follows established organizational hierarchy and structure (as described in a typical organizational chart, see Figure 5.1). This includes *downward communication* messages, sent from superordinates to subordinates to provide job instruction and goal indoctrination; *upward communication*, sent from subordinates to superordinates to provide bosses with feedback and to gain support for workers; and *horizontal communication*, sent between individuals on the same organizational level to facilitate task coordination and social support (Kreps 1990a). *Informal organizational communication* is not dictated by organizational hierarchy and structure but develops based on the natural development of interpersonal relationships between organizational actors. Informal organizational communication is often referred to as gossip or the "grapevine", but it serves important information dissemination and social functions for organizational participants.

Formal and informal channels are interdependent. The better the formal organizational channels are at providing organization members with relevant information, the less need there is for informal channels. Participants in organizational life have insatiable appetites for relevant organizational information. Yet, the formal channels rarely provide enough relevant information to satisfy this appetite for information. Informal channels of communication arise to provide the inside information that organizational actors desire that is not readily available via

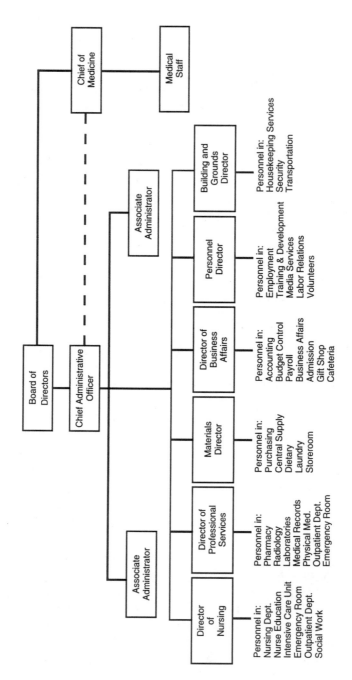

Figure 5.1. Organizational Chart for a Mythical Health Care Organization

SOURCE: Reprinted by permission of Waveland Press, Inc., from Gary L. Kreps and Barbara C. Thornton, *Health Communication: Theory and Practice, Second Edition*, p. 95. Copyright 1992 by Waveland Press, Inc., Prospect Heights, Illinois.

the formal communication system. Although some personal and political information may not be appropriate for dissemination via formal channels of organizational communication, the informal information system can usually accommodate the most sensitive, personal, and risky information. Unfortunately, informal channels of communication may not always carry the highest quality (full and accurate) information because informal leaders do not always have access to such information.

Interestingly, although informal channels of communication are not mandated and legitimized by the structure of the organization, they have several advantages over formal channels. They are less likely than formal channels of communication to distort information as it is passed through the organization. Formal channels of communication, especially upward and downward communication, often suffer from *serial transmission of information*, a one-way transmission of messages with little or no feedback that becomes increasingly distorted as the messages are passed from one person to another. As the messages are exchanged up or down the organizational hierarchy, the original message becomes more and more distorted because of inadvertent omissions, changes, and additions of relevant information.

Informal channels do not suffer from distortion as much as formal channels because organization members feel more free to seek feedback and clarification from informal contacts (usually friends) than they do from formal contacts (often bosses or subordinates), there are often multiple sources of information in informal channels (with particularly "juicy" information spreading like wildfire from many informal sources), and organizational actors often pay more attention to informal channels (which often carry "juicy" information) than they do to formal channels. When formal and informal channels do contradict each other, organization members are more likely to believe informal information sources than formal sources. In the best organizations, leaders attempt to coordinate the use of formal and informal channels of communication, so they complement each other, rather than contradict one another (Kreps, 1990a).

◆ Organizational Culture and Multicultural Relations

Every organization develops it own unique cultural identity, often referred to as its *corporate culture* or *organizational culture*. Organizational culture refers to the collectively held beliefs, values, and *interpretive logics* that organization members use to make sense of and respond to diverse phenomena. Just as in national, ethnic, and professional cultures, organizational cultures establish norms for member behaviors and influence the ways members see the world.

Systemwide organizational cultures are comprised of many subcultures. These subcultures often are constituted of several different cultural groups represented in the organization, such as groups composed of members who have similar educational backgrounds (holding the same MBA, PhD, MD, or RN degrees), members who work in the same functional area of the organization (accounting, surgery, pediatrics, or housekeeping), members who share the same racial, ethnic, or socioeconomic backgrounds, as well as members who may share similar activities (bowling league, executives club, or commuters).

Each subculture within the organizational culture represents a unique set of norms that dictates member beliefs, attitudes, and values. Every subculture has its own identity and has its own relative status within the organization. The organizational status of subcultures changes as the organization's political landscape evolves. At any given point in time some subcultures are more influential in the organization than others. Members of organizational subcultures often jockey for power and position within the organizational political structure, using communication as a primary political tool (Kreps, 1990a).

Political struggle is a common phenomenon in many organizations, where different subcultures compete for status and influence. In health care delivery organizations, subcultural competition can be clearly seen in strained interprofessional relations among health care providers and even in opposition between representatives of different departments. For example, members of a hospital Pediatrics Department may feel antagonistic toward members of the Obstetrics or Surgery Department because they are socialized to believe they are in direct competition with these departments for limited equipment, supplies, or personnel resources. Cultural ethnocentrism can lead to interdepartmental (and interprofessional) antagonism because the members of one subculture underestimate the legitimacy of other subcultures' claims for resources while overestimating the validity of their own resource demands. Such culturally based antagonisms are created by ineffective multicultural relations and can undermine the interdepartmental cooperation in hospitals and health care centers that is so necessary for effective health care delivery.

Effective multicultural communication can be used to offset this tendency toward ethnocentrism and subcultural competition in health care organizations. Since the organizationwide culture establishes norms for guiding competition between subcultures and helps create a climate for organizational receptivity to different cultural groups, communication can be used to guide the development of norms that promote multicultural receptivity and sensitivity. Organizational cultures, just like other cultures, are created and sustained through organizational communication. *Metacommunicative messages* (messages that provide feedback about the acceptability of previous communication strategies) can be used to establish norms that encourage members to respect one another (Kreps, 1990a). By providing continuous unanimous support to members for communicating in ways that demonstrate respect for cultural diversity, metacommunication can be used to enhance the normative structures of organizational cultures and promote effective multicultural relations in health care organizations (Kreps, 1993a).

◆ Communication Climates in Organizations

Communication climate (the emotional tone present within the organization) has a major influence on subcultural cooperation in organizational life. Just as the actual weather we

TABLE 5.1 Supportive and Defensive Communication Climates

Supportive Climates	Defensive Climates
1. Description	1. Evaluation
2. Problem Orientation	2. Control
3. Spontaneity	3. Strategy
4. Empathy	4. Neutrality
5. Equality	5. Superiority
6. Provisionalism	6. Certainty

SOURCE: Reprinted from Jack R. Gibb (1961), Defensive Communication, *Journal of Communication, 11*, p. 147.

encounter outdoors every day (hot, cold, rainy, snowy, or sunny) influences how we feel and behave, the communication climate within an organization (whether it is tense, confrontational, or relaxed) influences the ways organization members feel and behave.

Jack Gibb (1961) describes *communication climates* as ranging from being supportive to defensive (see Table 5.1). *Supportive climates* are ones in which organization members feel comfortable interacting and working with one another, fostering both collaboration and trust (Kreps & Thornton, 1992). The more supportive organizational climates are, the more likely organization members are to feel comfortable with other members and respect different cultural perspectives represented within the organization. Supportive climates encourage cooperation among organizational subcultures.

In defensive communication climates organization members feel uncomfortable with one another, are not disposed toward sharing relevant information, and are suspicious of one another. *Defensive climates* discourage cooperation and diminish the effectiveness of multicultural relations. "In health care, defensive climates are often characterized by blaming, time constraints, and a hierarchy that does not take individuals into consideration. They are judgmental, manipulative, emotionally neutral, and dogmatic. Unfortunately, most health related settings are defensive ones" (Kreps & Thornton, 1992, p. 69).

Communication climates are created by the kinds of communication behaviors and strategies used in organizational life. Gibb (1961) suggests that the more organizational actors communicate in ways that are cooperative, nonjudgmental, descriptive, candid, egalitarian, and flexible, the more likely they are to establish supportive organizational communication climates. Conversely, the more likely organizational actors are to communicate in ways that are overly critical, dominating, pre-planned, uncaring, superior, and dogmatic, the more likely they are to establish defensive organizational climates. Since supportive communication climates promote effective multicultural relations in health care organizations, it is important for those involved in the health care enterprise to engage in supportive communicative behaviors and strategies as often as possible.

◆ Weick's Model of Organizing and Cultural Diversity

Karl Weick (1979) in his model of organizing refers to the different situations and events that organizational actors encounter as *information inputs*, emphasizing the importance of information in organizational life. In fact, he suggests the primary reason for organizing is to provide individuals with support and feedback in responding to highly equivocal situations (information inputs). Thus, communication plays an important role in social organizing, by helping organizational actors cope with the challenges of interpreting and responding to equivocal information inputs.

Weick (1979) describes organizational environments as information environments. That is, the most salient feature of any organizational environment is the information value of the different situations (information inputs) organizational actors encounter. When organizational actors effectively interpret and respond to the many different information inputs they attend to (selected from the enormous population of potential information inputs that are available in organizational life), they are able to make sense of organizational life and direct the accomplishment of individual and collective goals.

Equivocality refers to the relative level of complexity, lack of predictability, and ambiguity one has in responding to a particular event (Kreps, 1990a). Highly equivocal phenomena are very challenging, because they are difficult to understand (Weick, 1979). Yet, organization members have insatiable appetites for meaning and strive to resolve high equivocality by making sense out of challenging information inputs such as cultural diversity.

Interestingly, equivocality is not merely a characteristic of an event (or information input) but rather is a characteristic of the individual's ability to perceive and respond to the event. That is, a situation is not inherently imbued with a certain level of equivocality. A situation that is of very high equivocality to one person may be quite simple for another person. It is the ability of the individual to effectively interpret a phenomenon that determines its level of equivocality. Therefore, multicultural relations may now be a very equivocal phenomenon for many organizational actors, but with some communication experience, training, and skill-building, the equivocality of multicultural relations can be reduced.

A primary goal in organizational life is to develop the ability (communicative processes) and interpretive resources (*organizational intelligence*) to enable organizational actors to interpret and respond effectively to a broad range of information inputs. In hospitals, for example, it is imperative that health care providers respond appropriately to the broad range of health problems presented by the many different consumers who seek health care. Hospitals develop organizational intelligence (policies, procedures, and strategies), based on past organizing experiences, to guide individualized health care treatment for the many different consumers seeking care.

Organizational actors, like all human beings, have an insatiable appetite for meaning, for understanding the many different people and events they encounter every day (Kreps, 1990a). Some of these events (highly equivocal information inputs) challenge their ability to interpret and respond to information inputs, thus challenging their ability to be in control and make sense of their organizational environments. Weick (1979) contends that organizational actors use two primary communicative responses to make sense of different information situations encountered—the use of rules and cycles.

Rules are preestablished organizational strategies for directing organizational responses to different frequently encountered situations, such as the use of form letters to respond to recurrent information requests or the use of organizational guidelines and policies to guide the accomplishment of specific routine tasks. *Cycles* are the use of patterns of interlocked communication behaviors organizational actors engage in for processing information inputs to make sense of different organizational situations. Cycles include problem-solving interaction among members of decision-making groups, the asking for and receiving of advice and counsel, or merely the consulting of different reference sources to make sense of difficult situations.

The appropriate use of rules and cycles to respond to situations of differing levels of equivocality is explained by the *principle of requisite variety*, which suggests that for organizing to be effective, the level of equivocality of any information situation encountered by the organization must be matched by the equivocality of the responses the organization composes to react to the situations. That is, the more complex the situation is, the more complex the response to that situation should be (and also the corollary principle that the less complex the situation is, the less complex the response should be).

Rules are generally less equivocal for organizational actors than cycles are. Rules are of low equivocality for organization members because they are preestablished and provide the actors with specific guidelines for responding to different organizational situations. Cycles are more complex and uncertain than rules because they are more emergent and evolutionary. It is uncertain how a communicative interaction will transpire and what kinds of responses organizational actors will get to different queries.

Rules are designed to help organizational actors respond to routine situations. They are not very helpful for responding to highly equivocal situations because the situations are too complex and idiosyncratic to be covered by pre-set rules. This is the reason why the overuse of bureaucratic rules and policies often exacerbates problems, miring already complex organizational situations in a sea of red tape.

Communication cycles are best suited to help organizational actors respond to highly equivocal situations. Each communication cycle removes some equivocality from a complex information situation. Eventually communication cycles help organizational actors reduce enough of the equivocality from these complex situations to enable them to develop new rules and use these rules for guiding organizational responses to these situations. Therefore, communication is the essential process in organizing. It is only through the use of communication cycles that the equivocality that makes complex organizational situations so difficult to respond to can be reduced, demystifying formerly complex organizational inputs into situations in which rules can be established and used.

Because issues concerning cultural diversity in modern health care often challenge organizational actors' abilities to interpret, predict, and control organizational life, multicultural relations in health care are often a highly equivocal organizational problem. According to Weick's model of organizing and the principle of requisite variety, the best way to respond to the complexities of multicultural relations in health care is to encourage organizational actors to engage in communication cycles to help them reduce the equivocality they experience to a manageable enough level that rules can be developed and used. We advocate the development of communication strategies, structures, and media in modern health care delivery systems to address and demystify the equivocality of multiculturalism for participants in the health care system. Conferences, workshops, training sessions, public lectures, discussion groups, ethics committee meetings, and the use of written and audiovisual educational materials concerning multicultural sensitivity and cooperation are examples of communication activities that can serve as effective communication cycles for reducing the equivocality many members of the health care community (health care providers, administrators, and consumers and their loved ones) experience when interacting in culturally diverse health care situations.

◆ Communication and Leadership

Leadership is perhaps the most important factor in promoting effective multicultural relations because leaders have a powerful influence on organizational culture. Leadership communication practices set the tone for cultural sensitivity in organizations. Do organizational leaders demonstrate through their communication that they value cultural diversity? Do they encourage others to respect cultural diversity? Have they established any specific programs, structures, or policies for promoting cultural diversity in their organizations? The answers to these questions will go a long way in explaining the relative quality of multicultural relations in health care delivery organizations.

Leaders in health care delivery organizations provide important role models for health care provision. They exemplify how health care staff are supposed to communicate with different consumers. This is especially important in demonstrating how staff should interact with consumers who have often received prejudicial treatment in health care, such as people with AIDS (Johnson & Hopkins, 1990; Lambert, 1991; Mondragon, Kirkman-Liff, & Schneller, 1991; Strauss, Fagerhaugh, Suczek, & Weiner, 1991; Treichler, 1987, 1988), the poor (Kosa & Zola, 1975), minorities (Hoppe & Heller, 1975; Martiney, 1978; Quesada & Heller, 1977; White, 1974), women (Chesler, 1972; Corea, 1977; Mendelsohn, 1981), and the elderly (Kreps, 1986; 1990b; Mendelson, 1974; Pegels, 1980; United States Senate Special Committee on Aging, 1974, 1975; Wood, 1989). For example, Kreps (1986) identifies five primary interrelated health communication problems confronting the elderly in seeking health care: "(1) their loss of social status within the health care system; (2) their loss of personal independence and control over their health care treatment; (3) limitations in the availability of health care services to the aged; (4) the growing alienation, loneliness, and boredom of the elderly within the health care system; and (5) the increase in fraud and misrepresentation in health care for the elderly" (p. 56). Leaders can help overcome these problems by communicating their respect for elderly health care consumers and their commitment to providing them with the best possible health care services. They can also institute specific policies and training programs to promote sensitive and effective health care for all consumers.

Leadership communication strongly influences the development of both organizational cultures and communication climates. *Charismatic leaders* (engaging leaders who dramatically communicate a vision of organizational life that followers believe in) establish and communicate clear organizational values and goals that become norms within organizational cultures. Leaders who make it clear that they value cultural diversity and will not tolerate prejudicial and ethnocentric communication in their organizations enhance multicultural relations by setting recognizable standards for multicultural communication. In addition, by communicating in a caring and sensitive manner with organization members, leaders can help establish supportive communication climates that discourage cultural competition and encourage cooperation.

6

Multicultural Communication
in Health Promotion

The stories begin—
Messages promoting health—
Through sight and through sound.

◆ Communication and Health Promotion

Promoting public health and preventing the spread of dangerous health risks is an integral health care function of communication in society. Whether we are focusing on the prevention and control of acquired immunodeficiency syndrome (AIDS) or violence in our neighborhoods, a fusion of theory and practice in multicultural communication is urgently needed (Maibach, Kreps, & Bonaguro, 1993). The critical elements are in place for a concerted effort to develop and implement disease prevention/health promotion efforts on a nationwide basis, and the implications of successful outcomes of such activities suggests an ever-increasing demand for health behavior scientists and clinicians (Weiss, 1985). As AIDS affects more minorities, women, and children, health care facilities have needed to develop cross-cultural training programs for service providers to be more sensitive to culturally diverse clients (Day, 1990).

The very concept of meaningful health differs among cultures (Dodd, 1991, pp. 57-58). One cultural group might conceive of health as a state of well-being that one takes responsibility for; another cultural group might view illness as punishment for past behaviors. Effective health promotion efforts must begin with a clear understanding of the cultural influences on health beliefs and practices of target audiences (Conner, 1989).

Besides the challenges inherent in cultural diversity, the health care market is undergoing tremendous changes. For example, Hospital Corporation of America was seen as "the wave of the future" a few years ago by some experts who predicted that it would be one of a half-dozen national megafirms delivering health care by the mid-1990s. It has since sold off some 104 hospitals and is among the giants who are struggling. However, regional hospitals that have targeted special needs are doing relatively well (Peters, 1987).

This chapter examines the role of communication in promoting public health in a multicultural milieu that calls for a diversity as well as a commonality of strategies to meet the needs of targeted audiences. It offers examples of situations that call for multicultural proficiency utilizing appropriate interpersonal messages as well as mediated messages.

◆ Diversity of Strategies

Health care delivery organizations that target and fulfill special needs appear to do well even when other seemingly powerful health care giants are diminishing (Peters, 1987). Although we discuss some of the media campaigns that use generalized communication strategies later in this chapter, here we begin by examining the effectiveness of targeting and fulfilling special audience needs by focusing on a diversity of communication strategies.

No matter how "rational" the goals of a health care campaign are, from family planning to organ donation, cultural roots run deep and will influence audience member interpretations of the campaign. Family planners in developing countries have found that introducing birth control techniques to the female population, wife or mother, often did not work without knowledge of the family power structure. In India, for example, the grandmother was the person who had the authority to instruct the women in such matters. In some Southeast Asian countries the husband, not the doctor, was to insert the intrauterine devices (Rogers, 1983).

In a study of organ donation Randall (1991) suggested that *cultural awareness* may well be the key to successful marketing approaches. In a Hispanic family, for example, although the father of the dead child (potential organ donor) may be the head of the family, it is the grandmother (or mother) who decides health-related matters, and therefore she would be the one to be approached. Blood relationships supersede legal ones in the Hispanic culture; the parents, not the spouse, of a deceased person would have the more salient opinion in such matters.

Cultural values affect the decision-making processes of health care professionals as well as consumers, as exemplified in a study comparing the ideologies implicit in the clinical and ecological vocational rehabilitation models (Albee, 1984). The study suggests that the values underlying the clinical model are consistent with American attachment to individualism and that those connected with the ecological model emphasize interdependence and the influence of a wide range of social, economic, and political factors. The study concluded that the two ideologies corresponded to the perceived interests of professionals and consumers of vocational rehabilitation (Albee, 1984).

Acculturation may also be a factor in certain risk behaviors. A recent study compared three groups of female subjects ($n = 657$) aged 14 to 49: non-Hispanic English speaking, English-speaking Hispanics, and Spanish-speaking women enrolled in an education course on AIDS transmission and prevention (Rapkin & Erickson, 1990). The study was to assess the role of acculturation in increasing the risk of contracting human immunodeficiency virus (HIV). The incidence of sexually transmitted diseases, multiple sex partners, and drug and alcohol abuse was lower among Spanish-speaking Hispanic subjects. Hispanic English speakers were intermediate in risk level, suggesting an influence of acculturation on risk behaviors (Rapkin & Erickson, 1990).

Cultural variables influence international responses to AIDS and require the development of culturally sensitive programs to educate relevant populations and influence human behavior to arrest the disease (Erickson, 1990). In a study that analyzed the impact of religion and cultural values on AIDS educational programs in Malaysia and the Philippines, the educational literature on AIDS prepared by public health agencies was analyzed for effectiveness and congruence within the dominant religious and cultural practices in each country (Osteria & Sullivan, 1991). It was suggested that achievement of the objectives of AIDS education would be improved by adapting the educational literature to the cultural values of each country.

International institutes such as the World Health Organization (WHO) have sent mental health missions to camps on the Thai-Cambodia border to implement strategies for preventing mental illness among refugees (Albee, 1983; Mattson, 1989; Williams & Berry, 1991). To achieve their objectives, WHO targets groups at three levels: (1) local community, (2) national, and (3) international. Effective health promotion strategies call for public health messages of prevention and treatment that are congruent with the messages of the targeted cultural groups, which incorporate the intrapersonal and relational levels of the cultures' communication systems.

◆ Commonality of Strategies

Social scientists agree that a person who is a proficient communicator in his culture does not necessarily transfer that proficiency to other cultures. Neither does someone who is diagnosed as mentally ill in one culture receive the same diagnosis in other cultures. Are there, however, qualities that may be considered pancultural, universal, or transcending cultural variability? Maslow's Hierarchy of Needs (1954) lists survival, safety, and social needs as three fundamental needs at the base of the pyramid. The more health promotion messages address fundamental concerns, the more commonality and congruity there are with multicultural groups. When it was discovered that AIDS was not limited to a small number of obscure cultural groups, that heterosexuals as well as homosexuals, infants as well as adults, sexually inactive as well as sexually active persons can and do fall victim to the disease, this knowledge struck a responsive chord.

◆ Media Campaigns

A communication scholar challenged the theory of the *two-step flow* or the dependence by the mass audience on local opinion leaders (Sykora, 1991). Easy access to media messages of global concern such as the Gulf War, AIDS, the Los Angeles racial riots, and issues in the presidential election enable each viewer to respond directly to the media messages and to a media opinion leader of one's choice—such as a columnist or commentator. This reaction to the media makes video and radio messages an attention-getting opportunity for public service announcements. During the summer, for example, stores combined their advertisements with tips for water safety. A beer commercial may have included a drink-but-don't-drive, designate-a-driver announcement. These messages addressed the safety needs in Maslow's hierarchy.

We have already discussed the fundamental importance of social relationships in the hierarchy of needs. Multicultural communication proficiency facilitates the development of supportive relationships. In California, the State Department of Health has a slogan that says, "Friends can be good medicine" (Fischer, 1983). Behind the slogan is a media campaign to convince people that they could be physically and psychologically healthier and live longer if they developed supportive social relationships.

It is not uncommon to spend $70,000 or more for the production of a 30-second video message. A video message, therefore, must be attention-getting and emotion-evoking and must appeal to fundamental needs. Many English-language public service announcements have been dubbed or subtitled into other languages, such as Spanish, Korean, Japanese, French, and Ilocano. Conversely, some messages produced in foreign languages have English subtitles for the children of immigrants who do not speak their parents' mother tongue (Esquivel & Kietel, 1990). Many video messages also are closed-captioned for persons who are deaf or have hearing impairments.

In many local communities the audiences are being exposed to public health messages on a multitude of problems—AIDS, drugs, alcoholism, prenatal care, child care, elder care, child/spouse abuse, homelessness, hunger, and mental health. Many of the messages contain a telephone number to encourage follow-up.

In Hawaii, where the cost of living is one of the highest in the nation, both parents in most families are employed, and in a number of cases, parents have several jobs apiece. Child care for "latch-key children" was a priority that legislators addressed, and the "A-Plus Program," an after-school program for these children for a nominal cost, has been in place for the second year. Many schools also have a breakfast program for children who need to be dropped off early by their parents, and many parents claim that their children enjoy the breakfasts at school more than they do at home. The breakfasts are creative—sometimes they even have pizza.

It took media campaigns, lobbying by parents and neighborhood groups, as well as a crusade by the lieutenant governor to get the A-Plus Program off the ground and to maintain it. The state superintendent of education rallied school principals to keep their schools open after school, and those who participated in the program were paid an overload of $1,000+ a month. The students were supervised in activities in culture and the arts, in athletics, as well as in scholarly work. This is a costly program that is a model of multicultural communication proficiency that resulted in protecting the children's safety needs, meeting their social needs, and providing opportunity for enhancement of their self-esteem. Video and radio messages focused on bringing the need for such a program to the public's attention. Support for the program was generated through interpersonal communication and neighborhood meetings at different schools. The beneficiaries of this program are from diverse ethnic groups—Caucasian, Hawaiian, Samoan, Japanese, Filipino, Korean, Black, Vietnamese, Hmong, Cambodian, and Puerto Rican. A formative evaluation will be conducted as an integral part of the program.

Another program that has addressed the survival needs of the community is the Economic Education Program conducted by the Department of Education and the University of Hawaii. This is a multicultural program that addresses fiscal problems in an informative and entertaining way through comic books, films, videotapes, skits, panels, and public forums.

Empowerment—health care providers and decision makers listening to input from consumers and acting on the information—enabled the passage of landmark legislation such as the Americans With Disabilities Act. To effectively address the basic needs for consumers' health, safety, fiscal security, and social support, health promotion messages must focus on commonalities among members of the target audience.

We can be effective in multicultural health promotion (1) if we identify the desired results or objectives (Maibach, Kreps, & Bonaguro, 1993) and (2) if we can describe the process of achieving these goals.

For example, what results do you want from the viewers or audience after you present the message? Would they learn about new health information? Would you be able to observe or measure this information gain? Would there be a change in their health-related beliefs, feelings, or attitudes? How would you observe or measure these changes? Would there be some action that would demonstrate the influences of the health promotion campaign? A new skill acquired or a behavioral change? Would you be able to observe or measure such a result?

Let's take the A-Plus Program. If members of the target television viewers or radio audience can identify the A-Plus Program and the needs it serves, they have met the cognitive objective (information gain). If they have an opportunity to express this information in the form of oral or written feedback, this result could be observed and measured.

If the audience were asked whether they were supportive of the program, they could express their response either orally or in written form. If this were done prior to the presentations, then there could be a pre-test and a post-test, and the difference could be measured. If a significant proportion of the audience responded favorably, then the affective objective (feelings and attitudes) would have been met. If the audience signed up to support the program and/or to enroll their children in the program, the psychomotor objective (action) would have been met.

The communication process describes the message and how it was presented. For example, what was the content of the message? Was it culture-sensitive? What was the general tone? How was the message presented? What medium was used? Were the nonverbal components such as body language and paralanguage appropriate for the situation? Did they show congruence? Did they evoke the desired response?

We recognize the importance of cultural variables in planning communication efforts. But are there any cultural universals? A group of journalism students from the University of California at Los Angeles were preparing for an audience with Pope John Paul. They asked an alumna who is a public relations specialist about the appropriate way to conduct themselves. The alumna consulted with a representative of the Vatican. His answer was, "Just be polite," suggesting that politeness is a universal cultural value (*UCLA Bulletin*, 1992). However, interpretations of what is "polite" and "impolite" behavior may vary from one culture to another.

In another intercultural situation, a Japanese-American who was visiting Japan for the first time was experiencing some anxiety in meeting her relatives in Hiroshima. Thoroughly

Westernized, she had traveled to Europe several times without any trepidation, but she was concerned about how she should behave in Japan. She consulted the president of the Japanese Cultural Center of Hawaii, a Japanese-American who had lived in Japan for a number of years. "Just be considerate," he advised.

Although we are warned not to oversimplify multicultural communication proficiency, there may be a cultural universal. Several years ago one of the authors of this book visited Swami Sarvagatananda at Cambridge, Massachusetts. Swami lectures on Eastern philosophy and religion at Harvard University and the Massachusetts Institute of Technology. "What have you learned?" he asked, offering her some apple juice in his library. "You must learn from everybody," he said, smiling. "Listen to them. Each person has so much to offer."

When PEACESAT (Pan Pacific Education and Communication Experiments by Satellite) connected Hawaii with the Pacific Islands—Papua New Guinea, Tonga, Samoa, and Rorotonga—all educational transmissions were to be done by mutual consent, with mutual respect. In order to transmit what the Pacific Islanders wanted—whether it was a presentation from the School of Medicine or the College of Social Sciences—the University of Hawaii listened to their input. In listening, the university presenters had the opportunity to ask questions and learn about the islanders' culture. It was a mutual interchange and empowered the audience as well as the presenters. Each interchange included objectives that were mutually agreed on, and an evaluation was conducted orally as well as through facsimile transmission. The objectives for the programs were generally met, and it seems that the following haiku could be a message of aloha for communicators who achieve mutual objectives:

> *'Neath whatever sun,*
> *May your drives through Life's fairway*
> *End as holes-in-one.*

◆ The Strategic Health Communication Campaign Model

Developing and implementing effective health communication campaigns is a deceivingly complex enterprise (Kreps,
1990c; Maibach, Kreps, & Bonaguro, 1993; Portnoy, Anderson,
& Ericksen, 1989). Health promotion campaign planners must
recognize that mere exposure to relevant health information
will rarely lead directly to desired health behavior changes (Edgar,
Hammond, & Freimuth, 1989; Tones, 1986). Maibach, Kreps,
and Bonaguro (1993) address the tenuous and complex relationship between communication efforts and health promotion in
their Strategic Health Communication Campaign Model that
identifies 5 major stages and 12 key issues a health promotion
campaign planner should consider in developing and implementing health promotion programs. (See Figure 6.1 for a depiction of the Strategic Health Communication Campaign Model.)

The first stage of the model is Planning, which addresses two
major issues: (1) setting clear and realistic *campaign objectives*,
and (2) establishing a clear *consumer orientation* to make sure
the campaign reflects the target audiences' specific concerns
and cultural perspectives. A consumer orientation means that
the whole campaign is designed from the unique cultural perspective of the target audience and members of the audience
are involved as much as possible in campaign planning and
implementation (Maibach, Kreps, & Bonaguro, 1993).

The second stage of the model is the Use of Theory in
directing health promotion efforts. Theory provides campaign
planners with strategies for designing, implementing, and evaluating communication campaigns. Maibach, Kreps, and Bonaguro
(1993) recommend the use of a wide range of different theories
to direct health promotion, but specifically emphasize the use
of *exchange theories* (Lefebvre & Flora, 1988) and *behavioral
theories* (Bandura, 1986; Maibach, 1993; Rogers, 1983) at multiple levels (for example, at individual, network, organizational,
and societal levels).

The third stage in the model is Communication Analysis,
which identifies three critical issues in designing health pro-

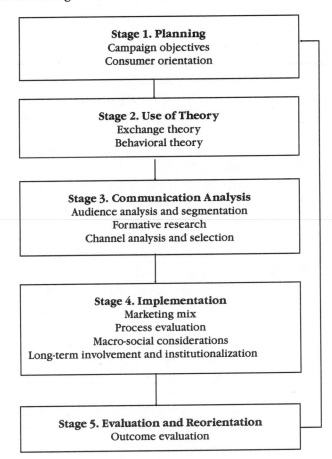

Figure 6.1. The Strategic Health Communication Campaign Model

SOURCE: Reprinted from Edward W. Maibach, Gary L. Kreps, and Ellen W. Bonaguro (1993), Developing strategic communication campaigns for HIV/AIDS prevention, in S. C. Ratzan (Ed.), *AIDS: Effective Health Communication for the 90s* (Washington, DC: Taylor & Francis, pp. 15-35), p. 19.

motion campaigns: (1) *audience analysis and segmentation*, (2) *formative research*, and (3) *channel analysis and selection*. Audience segmentation involves breaking down large culturally heterogeneous populations into smaller, more manageable, and more homogenous target audiences for health promotion campaigns (Kreps & Thornton, 1992). The greater the *cultural homogeneity* (the more they share cultural attributes and backgrounds) of a target audience, the better able campaign planners are to design health promotion messages specifically for them (Kotler & Roberto, 1989). After segmenting the target audience into the most culturally homogenous group possible, the campaign planner should gather as much information as possible about the group's relevant cultural norms, beliefs, values, and attitudes to guide the design of the campaign. The more complete the audience analysis process is, the more prepared the campaign planner is to tailor the health promotion messages to the specific needs and predilections of the target audience. Formative research is the process used to guide the design and development of the campaign by gathering relevant information about the target audience and their likely reactions to campaign messages. Formative research should also help campaign planners make knowledgeable choices about which communication channels to use in the campaign because they are most likely to reach and influence specific target audiences.

The fourth stage of the model is Implementation, which involves establishing an effective *marketing mix* for the campaign, evaluating the campaign process, identifying *macrosocial conditions* that may influence accomplishment of the campaign goals, and designing strategies for promoting long-term involvement and *institutionalization* of campaign activities with the target audience. Marketing mix (the 4 Ps: product, price, placement, and promotion) refers to establishing a clear set of campaign activities and media (products) that promote objectives audience members can adopt with minimal economic or psychological costs (price) that are presented in an attractive manner likely to reach the target audience (placement) and provide audience members with information about how, when, and where they can access campaign information and programs (promotion) (Kotler & Roberto, 1989; Maibach, Kreps, & Bonaguro, 1993). Process evaluation is used to keep track and evaluate campaign activities to identify areas for fine-tuning campaign communication efforts. Because target audiences reside within and are interdependent with the larger society, campaign planners must attempt to involve these larger social systems (such as business organizations and government agencies) in supporting and participating in campaign activities. Furthermore, to make sure that the campaign's health promotion goals and activities are fully implemented and established into the life of the target audience, the campaign planner should design strategies for the audience's long-term involvement with these activities and the institutionalization of these activities as a regular part of the consumers' daily life. An excellent strategy for such institutionalization is to empower target audience members to get personally involved with implementing and managing campaign programs so they have a greater stake in achieving campaign goals and the campaign activities become part of the audience's normative cultural activities.

The fifth and final stage of the strategic communication campaign model is Evaluation and Reorientation, in which a *summative evaluation* (evaluation of campaign outcomes) is conducted to determine the relative success of the campaign in achieving its goals at an acceptable cost as well as to identify areas for future health promotion interventions. The information gathered through such outcome evaluations reorients campaign planners to the unmet health needs of the target audience, inevitably leading campaign planners back to the first stage of the model (planning) where they identify new health promotion goals for future communication campaigns.

Obviously, culture plays a very important role in designing and implementing strategic health communication campaigns. The campaign planner must carefully examine the different cultural influences on public health behavior, analyze the specific cultural attributes of target audiences for health promotion efforts, design campaign programs and messages that fit the cultural orientations of members of the target audience, and institutionalize campaign goals and programs within the culture of the target audience. Only through sensitive and strategic multicultural communication campaign efforts can important health promotion goals be achieved.

7

Guidelines for Effective Multicultural Health Communication

Communication
Forms an ocean of oneness
From cultural seas.

◆ The Crisis of Culture in Modern Society

Modern life is currently in cultural turmoil and transition (Locke, 1992; Schlesinger, 1992). Although society is becoming increasingly multicultural, with increasing participation of individuals representing many different national, ethnic, racial, gender, and professional cultures in political, educational, business, and health care settings (Copeland, 1988; Lambrinos, 1992), uncertainty about how to communicate effectively across these different cultures has made modern life increasingly challenging (Geber, 1990). This is especially true for participants in the modern health care system, as we have illustrated throughout this book.

Cultural Segregation————► Naive Integration————► Pluralistic Integration

Figure 7.1. Cultural Ideologies

An examination of relevant literature and social trends suggests there is a historical pattern to the ways American society has responded to increasing cultural diversity (Schlesinger, 1992). We have identified three major *cultural ideologies* that have emerged over time as competing interpretive and behavioral frameworks for guiding the ways people respond to the equivocality of *cultural diversity*. These ideologies include the following (see Figure 7.1 for a depiction of these three cultural ideologies):

1. Cultural Segregation
2. Naive Integration
3. Pluralistic Integration

The earliest, and unfortunately perhaps the most prevalent, of these perspectives is the ideology of *cultural segregation*. This ideology emphasizes cultural dominance and separation between the dominant culture (usually the cultural group that has been around the longest or that controls the largest share of economic resources) and other "marginal" cultural groups (Schlesinger, 1991). In the ideology of segregation, the group that serves as the dominant culture dictates the cultural standards by which all members are judged. The dominant culture in the modern health care systems is often represented by white, male, well-educated, and wealthy individuals, although this may vary based on which cultures are numerically predominant or influential within the membership of a particular organization (Kanter, 1977). For example, Kreps (1987) reported an interesting study of reverse sexism in health care where female nurses were the dominant culture and male nurses belonged to a "marginal" culture within a large urban medical center.

The dominant culture establishes normative rules for accept-able behavior within social systems, forcing all members to either adopt these prescribed behaviors or be isolated, alienated, and punished. Within modern health care systems, such punish-ment often takes the form of limited access to relevant health information as well as decreased social influence and respect. Under this "melting pot" ideology individuals are encouraged to give up their own cultural identities and to the greatest extent possible adopt the cultural perspective of the dominant culture. *Metacommunication* is used to clearly demonstrate to members that it is to their long-term benefit to emulate the dominant culture if they want to succeed.

The ideology of segregation is based on *ethnocentrism*, where members of the dominant culture assume their cultural per-spective is "best" and other cultural orientations are inferior. This ethnocentric orientation has caused many problems in society (and in the modern health care system) by alienating individuals who are not members of the dominant culture, decreasing the exchange of relevant information between individuals from different cultural perspectives, and diminishing the extra en-ergy (*synergy*) that derives from multicultural cooperation.

The second cultural ideology to emerge is the ideology of *naive integration*, which purports to fully accept all cultural groups but, like the ideology of segregation, really emphasizes co-optation of the "marginal" cultures by dominant cultural groups. This ideology publicly espouses respect for different cultural perspectives, yet those in key decision making posi-tions invariably follow the ethnocentric dogma of the dominant culture. For example, token representatives of "marginal" cul-tural groups are often hired to visible positions within modern organizations to give the image of organizational pluralism but are rarely given much authority unless they denounce their cultural roots and adopt the dominant norm system. This naive integration ideology is all too prevalent in modern health care systems, and it causes as many problems as the ideology of segregation because like the ideology of segregation it under-mines multicultural synergy. Naive integration is even more sinister than the ideology of segregation because it falsely purports to respect cultural diversity, giving culturally diverse groups the false expectation of equity and opportunity.

The newest cultural ideology to emerge, and the one that we advocate in this book, is *pluralistic integration*. In the ideology of pluralistic integration, respect is shown for cultural diversity, members of different cultural groups are encouraged to retain and express their cultural perspectives, and social systems reap the benefits of having members share relevant information, eliciting both cooperation and synergy. This ideology is difficult to implement because it depends on using communication to establish and maintain effective multicultural relations. Therefore, competent and sensitive communication is the key to pluralistic integration and effective multicultural relations in health care contexts.

◆ Recommendations for Promoting Effective
Multicultural Relations in Health Care Contexts

Throughout this book we have identified and analyzed a broad range of challenges to effective multicultural relations confronting participants in the modern health care system. In examining these challenges we have also identified many communication strategies for enhancing multicultural relations and health care delivery. In this final section, we summarize some of the major recommendations we have reached (92 suggestions in all) for promoting effective multicultural relations in health care.

Be aware, however, in reviewing our suggestions that these recommendations are not mutually exclusive of one another but build on one another and interact in many ways to form a unified configuration of strategies for developing multicultural health communication competencies and promoting public health. You should also realize that this is not a complete list of recommendations for multicultural health communication effectiveness. There is much we still need to learn about the complexities of human communication in health care. Our incomplete knowledge prevents us from presenting an exhaustive list of recommendations. These concluding ideas should be seen as potentially fruitful starting points for enhancing multicultural relations in health care contexts and promoting public health. So, based on our best recommendations (from the preceding six chapters), we encourage participants in the modern health care system to do the following:

1. Be aware that although some of an individual's cultural influences may be readily apparent, others are hidden and may not be immediately recognized in initial interactions. To promote effective multicultural relations we must get to know the individuals we interact with so we can identify the salient, yet hidden, cultural factors that can have major influences on communication and cooperation in health care contexts.

2. Be aware that developing effective multicultural relationships between culturally unique participants in the modern health care system is a prerequisite to effective health care delivery. So we should work toward developing cooperative interpersonal relationships with the people we interact with in health care.

3. Be aware that attempts to force others to give up their personal culturally approved beliefs and behaviors can lead to anger and resentment and is a common reason for ineffective communication in health care. So we encourage you to resist tendencies to act ethnocentrically (seeing your cultural perspective as the only legitimate point of view) and avoid attempts to proselytize others (forcing others to adopt your cultural perspective and give up their own), demonstrating respect, tolerance, and acceptance of divergent ideas and perspectives.

4. Develop and express genuine interest and respect for different cultural orientations. Not only should we be tolerant of different cultural perspectives, we should demonstrate active interest and admiration for the cultural norms of other cultures.

5. Explore different cultures to help you learn about new ways of interpreting reality, increasing your understanding of other people, their experiences, and the world they live in.

Therefore, we encourage participants in the modern health care system to become students of different cultures to learn about the cultural norms and significant symbols that influence those they interact with. We must work to overcome communication barriers, to understand different languages, rituals, logics, and norms.

6. Be aware that there are many different legitimate perspectives on and interpretations of reality, as well as many different ways to solve problems. We encourage you to get to know others from different cultural orientations in order to gather new information from these divergent cultural perspectives, ultimately benefiting from the theory of weak ties.

7. Be aware that to communicate effectively with those who are culturally dissimilar to us, we must be willing to endure the discomfort of unfamiliarity and uncertainty. We must be open-minded and receptive, developing both patience and a high tolerance for ambiguity.

8. Be aware that health care treatment must attend to both the physical and symbolic aspects of illness to be effective. We encourage you to communicate to learn about the different culturally based health beliefs, values, and attitudes that influence relevant others' interpretations of health and health care, eliciting information about their symbolic interpretations of illness and providing relevant information and feedback about these interpretations to help both consumers and providers make sense out of health care.

9. Engage in effective multicultural communication with the many different consumers you encounter in the modern health care system to help them overcome the limitations imposed by the sick role through establishing meaningful and supportive interpersonal relationships, eliciting cooperation from relevant others, and gathering pertinent information to enable them to actively participate in directing their health care.

10. Develop effective multicultural relationships to help members of the health care community resist the many stressors that are likely to derive from working interdependently with so many individuals representing different cultural groups. By

avoiding the dissonance and stress caused by tense multicultural relations in health care contexts, individuals are able to help balance their complex body chemistry, protecting their physical and psychological health. In this way, effective multicultural communication acts to promote personal health.

11. Develop communication attitudes and skills that demonstrate an appreciation and sensitivity to cultural diversity that will enable participants in the modern health care system to avoid the many physical and psychological perils associated with culture shock.

12. Enhance personal health by developing skills in accessing, processing, disseminating, and evaluating information; managing feelings and attitudes; and acquiring competent intercultural communication skills and behaviors. This multicultural communication proficiency enables one to communicate effectively with people of different backgrounds in expressing one's needs, to learn about others, and to adapt to the many constraints of life. It enables one to obtain information from health care providers and consumers in diverse cultural settings.

13. Develop the collective spirit of *ohana*, which clearly exemplifies the effective use of multicultural communication to build meaningful interpersonal relationships and establish solidarity between individuals from disparate cultural orientations and backgrounds.

14. Implement and use intercultural communication training programs for participants in the modern health care system as an organizational intervention to promote the development of multicultural communication competencies and to create a more conducive climate in health care delivery organizations.

15. See yourself as a change agent during multicultural interactions by monitoring communication situations, obtaining data through your observations, listening reflectively and empathetically, and using this information to transmit appropriate verbal and nonverbal messages that empower relational partners to produce mutually desired results in health management.

16. Do not prejudicially limit your examination and selection of health care treatments based on ethnocentric preference for

traditional health care methods but endeavor to review the wide range of traditional and alternative courses of treatment available, which will enable you to determine the best therapies for the individual health care problems you are attempting to address.

17. Establish and maintain clear implicit contracts for coordinating activities in the health care enterprise.

18. Maintain effective interpersonal relationships by using your interpersonal communication to update implicit contracts, continually identifying relational partners' emergent expectations, letting these relational partners know that you intend to meet their expectations, and sharing your own expectations with relational partners.

19. Continually attempt to increase the number of different cultural groups you interact with. The greater the number of diverse groups one can communicate with successfully to achieve results in information gain, attitude change or reinforcement, and skill acquisition or behavior change, the greater the reduction in uncertainty and stress

20. When interacting in high-context cultures, you can reduce uncertainty by recognizing that members of these cultures are likely to follow group or cultural norms.

21. When interacting in low-context cultures, you should focus on individual behaviors, rather than group norms.

22. Be aware that knowing someone's background or having mutual friends may reduce uncertainty for members of high-context cultures. Therefore, not having contact with strangers' communication networks before the initial interaction increases uncertainty for high-context cultures, but not for low-context cultures in which norms provide much less information.

23. Be aware that being unable to empathize with strangers will increase uncertainty in high-context cultures, but not in low-context cultures.

24. Be aware that lack of knowledge about a stranger's background will increase uncertainty in high-context cultures, but not in low-context cultures.

25. Be aware of both the content and relationship implications of your messages to relational others.

26. Provide your relational partners with personal messages (as opposed to object messages) that are sensitive to cultural differences, validate relational others' cultural expectations, and enhance relationship development.

27. Attempt to coordinate and articulate your use of verbal and nonverbal messages in interpersonal interactions to promote understanding and avoid relational difficulties in health care.

28. Be aware that interpersonal interactants seem to need a certain amount of redundancy in communication to enhance predictability, reduce entropy, and help them maintain a comfortable psychological state.

29. Enhance interpersonal communication over the telephone by emphasizing appropriate paralinguistic nonverbal components of speaking, such as pitch, loudness, conversational speed, and voice quality, to influence the feelings and attitudes of the listeners. Multicultural training programs for distance communication often address this need to use paralinguistic messages to develop the relational aspect of telecommunications.

30. Focus on the specific messages sent by other participants in the health care system to understand what they are saying, rather than stereotyping them based on their cultural background.

31. Empower other participants in the health care system by demonstrating respect for them, listening carefully to what they say, and acting on their requests based on what you hear.

32. As a health care practitioner, provide your clients with full and accurate information, in a manner in which the consumer can understand, about what they can expect from health care treatment, allowing them to make knowledgeable choices about treatment and fulfilling the obligation of informed consent.

33. Use the following communication strategies to reduce uncertainty in multicultural relationships: passive—unobtrusive observation; active—no direct contact, asking third parties; and interactive—obtaining information directly.

34. Unobtrusively observe the nonverbal behaviors of those you interact with in the health care system to gather important cues about their feelings and needs.

35. Ask third parties to provide input when relational partners have difficulty articulating their problems, such as in cases of a language problem, dementia, or apprehension.

36. If you will be living or working in a culture different from your own, undergo culture-specific training. Such training should help you to become more flexible in inferring motives or attributing meaning to another's behavior, thus increasing their proficiency in multicultural communication.

37. Develop a personal style of interpersonal communication that strengthens your relationships and is mutually empowering.

38. Be aware that in effective health care groups, members develop cooperative interpersonal relationships based on the mutual agreements they have established to follow each other's directives.

39. Be aware that in addition to using communication to coordinate activities, group members use communication to provide one another with relevant information for accomplishing group goals.

40. When serving as a member of a health care group, be sure to share any relevant information you may possess about issues facing the group to help the group accomplish both task and socioemotional goals.

41. Use multicultural communication to encourage other group members to express their different points of view, helping to provide the group with a range of ideas that can shed insights into complex issues and identify alternative courses of group action.

42. Always recognize consumers of health care as a central part of any health care team.

43. Because evidence has demonstrated that consumer involvement in health care decision making often improves physical response to treatment, encourage clients to participate actively in making decisions concerning their care.

44. As a provider, use the opportunity to interact with clients within health care teams to learn more about the needs and experiences of these consumers. The information gathered in team discussions can be used to guide health care treatment strategies.

45. As a consumer, participate actively and assertively in health care teams to learn more about health care treatment strategies, enabling you to make well-informed choices about treatment.

46. As a member of a health care team, minimize interprofessional cultural biases and communicate egalitarianly for your health care team to be effective.

47. Use ethics committees to help health care delivery organizations evaluate the moral issues involved in making decisions about many complex situations, such as when to provide treatment to or withhold it from a terminally ill patient, when to use or discontinue use of placebo drugs with clinical trial research subjects who are seriously ill and are likely to benefit from established medications, or which patient among many seriously ill applicants on a waiting list for a heart transplant should receive the next available donated organ.

48. Make sure that ethics committees carefully deliberate the issues concerning complex moral dilemmas in health care and examine available options and the implications of different courses of action for all parties concerned, ultimately providing health care administrators with evaluations of the issues to guide decision making and to set policies for guiding future actions. These committees' determinations about ethical courses of action must take relevant cultural orientations into account.

49. Make sure that ethics committee interaction demonstrates respect for the different cultural perspectives and encourages group members to actively share their cultural experiences in the group evaluations of ethical issues. Effective multicultural relations among the members of ethics committees are essential to enabling these groups to engage in effective deliberation of bioethical issues.

50. Make sure that ethics committees seek relevant information from sources external to the committee, taking into account the relevant cultural perspectives of all individuals involved in the issues under examination, to fully evaluate bioethical decisions and courses of action.

51. See that social support groups help their members cope with life stress through communication, by providing them with relevant information about health care methods and services, problem solving interaction, referral services, friendly visits, and assistance in making choices about health care options available to them. These groups should help members feel good about themselves and assert control of their own health care.

52. Be sure that modern health care delivery organizations promote effective multicultural relations among their many different interdependent staff members, providers, and consumers.

53. Be aware that to accomplish the related goals of health promotion and preservation, health care organizations depend on cooperation and coordination among interdependent health care providers, health care administrators, staff members, and consumers to effectively provide health care services.

54. Be sure that modern health care organizations deemphasize status differences and distance between providers and consumers, to minimize cultural distance between providers and consumers in order to promote the sharing of relevant cultural information in health care.

55. See that health care delivery organizations use communication to coordinate activities at multiple organizational levels. Communication is used both to facilitate cooperation among members of the same organizations and to elicit cooperation among representatives of different organizations.

56. See that health care delivery organizations use sensitive multicultural message strategies in internal communication to perform important administrative functions such as providing job instructions, directing task accomplishment, and providing performance evaluation.

57. See that health care delivery organizations use sensitive multicultural message strategies in external communication to

establish good public relations with members of the relevant environment by providing these external publics with relevant information (such as annual reports, health education publications, press releases, or advertisements), gathering information about external issues of relevance to the organization, and promoting coordination between the organization and key members of its relevant environment.

58. See that health care delivery organizations effectively coordinate internal and external channels of organizational communication to maintain an often precarious, yet critically important, balance between innovation and stability in organizational life.

59. Be sure that health care delivery organizations use relative openness to match their use of internal and external communication to the source (internal or external) and extent of information turbulence (which is often caused by strained multicultural relations).

60. Use internal and external channels of communication to demonstrate respect for and encourage the sharing of culturally diverse ideas and interpretations of organizational reality, encouraging the use of multicultural interaction in creative problem solving and innovation generation in organizational life.

61. Be sure that health care delivery organizations use internal organizational communication to promote cultural convergence by establishing new organizationally based cultural norms for guiding coordination among organization members.

62. As leaders of health care delivery organizations, you should attempt to coordinate the use of formal and informal channels of organizational communication so they complement each other, rather than contradict each other.

63. Use effective multicultural communication to offset the tendency for ethnocentrism and subcultural competition in health care organizations. Since the organizationwide culture establishes norms for guiding competition between subcultures and helps create a climate for organizational receptivity to different cultural groups, communication can be used to guide

the development of norms that promote multicultural receptivity and sensitivity.

64. To provide continuous unanimous support to members for communicating in ways that demonstrate respect for cultural diversity, use metacommunication to enhance the normative structures of organizational cultures and promote effective multicultural relations in health care organizations.

65. Engage in supportive communicative behaviors and strategies as often as possible. This is important for those involved in the health care enterprise, because supportive communication climates promote effective multicultural relations in health care organizations.

66. Be sure that health care delivery organizations endeavor to develop and preserve organizational intelligence (policies, procedures, and strategies), based on past organizing experiences, to guide individualized health care treatment for the many different consumers seeking care.

67. Engage in communication cycles in order to help reduce the equivocality of multicultural relations in health care contexts so that the equivocality can be lessened to a manageable enough level that rules can be developed and used. We advocate the development of communication strategies, structures, and media in modern health care delivery systems to address and demystify the equivocality of multiculturalism. Conferences, workshops, training sessions, public lectures, discussion groups, ethics committee meetings, and the use of written and audiovisual educational materials concerning multicultural sensitivity and cooperation are examples of communication activities that can serve as effective communication cycles.

68. As a leader in a health care delivery system, you should demonstrate through your communication that you value cultural diversity and encourage others to respect cultural diversity. Establish specific programs, structures, and policies for promoting cultural diversity in your organization.

69. As a leader in a health care delivery organization, you should exemplify how health care staff are supposed to communicate with different consumers, demonstrating how staff

should interact with consumers who have often received prejudicial treatment in health care, such as people with AIDS, the
poor, minorities, women, and the elderly.

70. Communicate in a caring and sensitive manner with
organization members. As a leader, you can help establish supportive communication climates that discourage cultural competition and encourage cooperation.

71. Be sure that health promotion efforts begin with a clear
understanding of the cultural influences on health beliefs and
practices of the target audiences. This will help the efforts be
effective.

72. Be aware that no matter how "rational" the goals of a
health care campaign are, from family planning to organ donation, cultural roots run deep and will influence audience member interpretations of the campaign.

73. Be aware that cultural variables influence international
responses to health and health care and require the development of culturally sensitive programs to educate relevant populations and influence health behaviors.

74. Be aware that effective health promotion strategies call
for public health messages of prevention and treatment that are
congruent with the messages of the targeted cultural groups,
which incorporate the intrapersonal and relational levels of the
cultures' communication systems.

75. Be aware that the more health promotion messages address fundamental concerns, the more commonality and congruity there are with multicultural groups.

76. Because of the expense of video production and dissemination, video health promotion messages must be attention-
getting and emotion-evoking and must appeal to fundamental
audience needs.

77. Remember that effective multicultural health promotion
efforts identify the desired results or objectives and describe
the process of achieving these goals.

78. Be aware that mere exposure to relevant health information will rarely lead directly to desired health behavior changes.

79. Remember that health communication campaigns should set clear and realistic *campaign objectives* and establish a clear *consumer orientation.*

80. Be sure that health communication planners use theory to guide their programs, because theory provides them with strategies for designing, implementing, and evaluating communication campaigns.

81. Be sure that campaign planners carefully segment target audiences, establishing a high level of cultural homogeneity to enhance their ability to develop campaign messages that are relevant to these audiences.

82. Be sure that campaign planners engage in extensive audience analysis to learn about target audiences and segmentation.

83. Be sure that campaign planners use formative research to evaluate and refine campaign strategies and programs.

84. Be sure that campaign planners carefully analyze and select communication channels that are likely to reach and influence members of the target audience.

85. Be sure that campaign planners carefully analyze how macrosocial conditions may influence accomplishment of the campaign goals.

86. Be sure that campaign planners design strategies for promoting long-term target audience involvement and institutionalization of campaign activities.

87. Be sure that campaign planners establish a clear set of campaign activities and media (products) that promote objectives that audience members can adopt with minimal economic or psychological costs (price) that are presented in an attractive manner that is likely to reach the target audience (placement) and provide audience members with information about how, when, and where they can access campaign information and programs (promotion).

88. Be sure that campaign planners use process evaluation to keep track of and evaluate campaign activities and identify areas for fine-tuning campaign communication efforts.

89. Be sure that campaign planners attempt to involve larger social systems (such as business organizations and government agencies) in supporting and participating in campaign activities.

90. Be sure that campaign planners design strategies for the audience's long-term involvement with campaign activities and the institutionalization of campaign activities and goals as a regular part of the consumers' daily life.

91. Be sure that campaign planners evaluate campaign outcomes to determine the relative success of the campaign in achieving its goals at an acceptable cost as well as to identify areas for future health promotion interventions.

92. Be sure that campaign planners carefully examine the different cultural influences on public health behavior, analyze the specific cultural attributes of target audiences for health promotion efforts, design campaign programs and messages that fit the cultural orientations of members of the target audience, and institutionalize campaign goals and programs within the culture of the target audience. Only through sensitive and strategic multicultural communication campaign efforts can important health promotion goals be achieved.

References

Albee, G. W. (1982a). Preventing psychopathology and promoting human potential. *American Psychologist, 37*(9), 1043-1050.

Albee, G. W. (1982b). A brief historical perspective on the primary prevention of childhood mental disorders. *Journal of Children in Contemporary Society, 14*(2-3), 3-12.

Albee, G. W. (1983). A comparison of refugees using and not using a psychiatric service: An analysis of DSM-III criteria and self-rating scales in cross-cultural context. *Journal of Operational Psychiatry, 14*(1), 38-41.

Albee, G. W. (1984). Ideologies of clinical and ecological models. *Rehabilitation Literature, 45*(11-12), 349-353.

Albee, G. W. (1985a). *The primary prevention of psychopathology*. Lecture presented at the University of Hawaii School of Medicine.

Albee, G. W. (1985b). From Vermont to Washington. *American Psychologist, 40*(2), 202-204.

Albee, G. W. (1985c). The contributions of clinical psychology to strategies for the primary prevention of psychopathology. *Bulletin of the Hong Kong Psychological Society, 15*, 7-23.

Albee, G. W. (1988). Toward a just society: Lessons from observations on the primary prevention of psychopathology. *American Psychologist, 41*(8), 91-98.

Albee, G. W., & Joffe, J. M. (Eds.). (1977). *The issues: An overview of primary prevention*. Hanover, NH: University Press of New England.

Albrecht, T., & Adelman, M. (1987). *Communicating social support*. Newbury Park, CA: Sage.

Alfidi, R. (1971). Informed consent: A study of patient reaction. *Journal of the American Medical Association, 216*, 1325-1329.

Arntson, P., & Droge, D. (1987). Social support in self help groups: The role of communication in enabling perceptions of control. In T. Albrecht & M. Adelman (Eds.), *Communicating social support* (pp. 148-171). Newbury Park, CA: Sage.

Ballard-Reisch, D. (1990). A model of participative decision-making for physician-patient interaction. *Health Communication, 2*, 91-104.

Ballard-Reisch, D. (1993). Health care providers and consumers making decisions together. In B. C. Thornton & G. L. Kreps (Eds.), *Perspectives on health communication* (pp. 66-80). Prospect Heights, IL: Waveland Press.

Bandura, A. (1986). *Social foundations of thought and action: A social cognitive approach.* Englewood Cliffs, NJ: Prentice Hall.

Barnlund, D. C. (1976). The mystification of meaning: Doctor-patient encounters. *Journal of Medical Education, 51*, 716-725.

Bastien, J. W. (1987). Cross-cultural communication between doctors and peasants in Bolivia. Special issue: Beyond the cure: Anthropological inquiries in medical theories and epistemologies. *Social Science and Medicine, 24*(12), 1109-1118.

Becker, M. (1974). The health belief model and personal health behavior. *Health Education Monographs, 2*, 409-419.

Benne, K., & Sheats, P. (1948). Functional roles of group members. *Journal of Social Issue, 4*, 41-49.

Benson, H. (1979). *The mind-body effect.* New York: Simon & Schuster.

Berrien, F. K. (1968). *General and social systems.* New Brunswick, NJ: Rutgers University Press.

Berrien, F. K. (1976). A general systems approach to organizations. In M. Dunnette (Ed.), *Handbook of industrial and organizational psychology.* Chicago, IL: Rand-McNally.

Bertalanffy, L. (1968). *General system theory.* New York: Braziller.

Bolton, R. (1986). *People skills.* New York: Simon & Schuster.

Bosford, B. (1986). *Bioethics committees.* Rockville, MD: Aspen.

Boyer, L., Lee, D., & Kirschner, C. (1977). A student run course in interprofessional relations. *Journal of Medical Education, 52*, 183-189.

Brislin, R. W. (1981). *Cross-cultural encounters: Face-to-face interaction.* New York: Pergamon.

Brown, I. C. (1963). *Understanding other cultures.* Englewood, NJ: Prentice Hall.

Burgoon, M., Parrott, R., Burgoon, J. K., Birk, T., Pfau, M., & Coker, R. (1987). Primary care physicians' selection of verbal compliance-gaining strategies. *Health Communication Journal, 2*(1), 13-27.

Burner, O. Y., Cunningham, P., & Hattar, H. S. (1990). Managing a multicultural nursing staff in a multicultural environment. *Journal of Nursing Administration, 20*(6), 30-34.

Campbell, R., & Chenoweth, B. (1981). *Peer support for older adults.* Ann Arbor, MI: University of Michigan Press.

Chesler, P. (1972). *Women and madness.* New York: Avon.

Chiraboga, D., Coho, A., Stein, J., & Roberts, J. (1979). Divorce, stress, and social supports: A study in help seeking behavior. *Journal of Divorce, 3*, 121-135.

Cline, R. W. (1990). Small group communication in health care. In E. Berlin Ray & L. Donohew (Eds.), *Communication and health: Systems and applications* (pp. 69-91). Hillsdale, NJ: Erlbaum.

Cluck, G., & Cline, R. (1986). The circle of others: Self help groups for the bereaved. *Communication Quarterly, 34*, 306-325.

Cohen, J., Sullivan, M., & Branehog, I. (1988). Psychosocial responses to cancer in California and Western Sweden: A comparative study. Special issue: Clinical research issues in psychosocial oncology. *Journal of Psychosocial Oncology, 6*(3-4), 25-40.

Condon, J. C., & Yousef, F. (1975). *An introduction to intercultural communication.* Indianapolis: Bobbs-Merrill.

Conner, R. F. (1989). A cross-cultural assessment of health promotion/disease prevention programs. *Evaluation and Program Planning, 11*(2), 179-187.

Copeland, L. (1988). Learning to manage a multicultural workforce. *Training, 25*(5), 48-56.

Corea, G. (1977). *The hidden malpractice: How American medicine treats women as patients and professionals.* New York: William Morrow.

Costello, D., & Pettegrew, L. (1979). Health communication theory and research: An overview of health organizations. In D. Nimmo (Ed.), *Communication yearbook 3* (pp. 607-623). New Brunswick, NJ: Transaction Press.

Cousins, N. (1979). *Anatomy of an illness as perceived by the patient.* New York: Norton.

Crane, D. (1975). The social potential of the patient: An alternative to the sick role. *Journal of Communication, 25*, 131-139.

Dass, R., & Gorman, P. (1985). *How can I help?* New York: Random House.

Day, N. A. (1990). Training providers to serve culturally different AIDS patients. Special issue: AIDS: Clinical perspective. *Family and Community Health, 13*(2), 46-53.

Dean, A., & Lin, N. (1977). The stress buffering role of social support. *The Journal of Nervous and Mental Disease, 165*(6), 403-417.

Dodd, C. H. (1991). *Dynamics of intercultural communication.* Dubuque, IA: William C. Brown.

Edgar, T., Hammond, S. L., & Freimuth, V. S. (1989). The role of the mass media and interpersonal communication in promoting AIDS-related behavioral change. *AIDS and Public Policy Journal, 4*, 3-9.

Elliot, G. R., Hamburg, D. A., & Parron, D. L. (Eds.) (1982). *Health and behavior.* Washington, DC: National Academy.

Erickson, R. J. (1990). International behavioral responses to a health hazard: AIDS. *Social Science and Medicine, 31*(9), 951-962.

Esquivel, G. B., & Kietel, M. A. (1990). Counseling immigrant children in the schools. *Elementary School Guidance and Counseling, 24*(3), 213-221.

Festinger, L. (1957). *A theory of cognitive dissonance.* Evanston, IL: Row, Peterson.

Fischer, C. (1983). The friendship cure-all. *Psychology Today, 17*, 24.

Frank, L. (1961). Interprofessional communication. *American Journal of Public Health, 51*, 1798-1804.

Freidson, E. (1970). *Professional dominance: The social structure of medical care.* Chicago, IL: Aldine.

Geber, B. (1990). Managing diversity. *Training, 27*(7), 23-30.

Geertz, C. (1973). *The interpretation of culture.* New York: Basic Books.

Gibb, J. (1961). Defensive communication. *Journal of Communication, 11*, 141-148.

Gifford, C. J. (1983, April). *Health team literature: A review and application with implications for communication research*. Paper presented to the Eastern Communication Association conference, Ocean City, MD.

Gill, M. S. (1993, July). New ways to health. *McCall's*, pp. 63-66.

Gochman, D. (1972). The development of health beliefs. *Psychological Reports, 31*, 259-266.

Granovetter, M. (1973). The strength of weak ties. *American Journal of Sociology, 78*, 1360-1380.

Greenfield, S., Kaplan, S., & Ware, J. E. (1985). Expanding patient involvement in care: Effects on patient outcomes. *Annals of Internal Medicine, 102*, 520-528.

Griffin, E. (1991). *A first look at communication theory*. New York: McGraw-Hill.

Gudykunst, W. B. (1988). Uncertainty and anxiety. In Y. Y. Kim & W. B. Gudykunst (Eds.), *Theories in intercultural communication* (pp. 123-156). Newbury Park, CA: Sage.

Gudykunst, W. B. (1993). Toward a theory of effective interpersonal and intergroup communication: An anxiety/uncertainty management (AUM) perspective. In R. L. Wiseman & J. Koester (Eds.), *Intercultural communication competence* (pp. 33-71). Newbury Park, CA: Sage.

Gudykunst, W. B., & Kim, Y. Y. (1992). *Communicating with strangers: An approach to intercultural communication* (2nd ed.). New York: McGraw-Hill.

Gudykunst, W. B., Ting-Toomey, S., & Chua, E. (1988). *Culture and interpersonal communication*. Newbury Park, CA: Sage.

Heiney, S., & Wells, L. (1989). Strategies for organizing and maintaining successful support groups. *Oncology Nursing Forum, 16*, 803-809.

Heisenhelder, J. B., & LaCharite, C. L. (1989). Fear of contagion: A stress response to acquired immunodeficiency syndrome. *Advances in Nursing Science, 11*(2), 29-38.

Helman, C. G. (1990). *Culture, health, and illness* (2nd ed.). London: Wright.

Hill, S. K. (1978). Health communication: Focus on interprofessional communication. *Communication Administration Bulletin, 25*, 31-36.

Hoppe, S., & Heller, P. (1975). Alienation, familism, and the utilization of health services by Mexican-Americans. *Journal of Health and Social Behavior, 16*, 304-314.

Horowitz, A. (1977). Social networks and pathways to psychiatric treatment. *Social Forces, 56*, 86-105.

Howe-Murphy, R., Ross, H., Tseng, R., & Hartwig, R. (1989). Effecting change in multicultural health promotion: A systems approach. *Journal of Allied Health, 18*(3), 291-305.

Illich, I. (1976). *Medical nemesis*. New York: Pantheon Press.

Infante, D. A. (1988). *Arguing constructively*. Prospect Heights, IL: Waveland Press.

Ingelfinger, F. (1972). Informed (but uneducated) consent. *New England Journal of Medicine, 287*, 465-466.

Johnson, W. B., & Hopkins, K. R. (1990). *The catastrophe ahead: AIDS and the case for a new public policy*. New York: Praeger.

Joy, R. O. (1987). Today's business world demands multicultural and international communication skills. *Business Education Forum, 41*(6), 27-30.

Kanter, R. M. (1977). *Men and women of the corporation.* New York: Basic Books.

Kavanaugh, K. H., & Kennedy, P. H. (1992). *Promoting cultural diversity: Strategies for health care professionals.* Newbury Park, CA: Sage.

Kim, Y. Y. (1991). Communication and adaptation. In L. Samovar & R. Porter (Eds.), *Intercultural communication: A reader* (6th ed., pp. 383-391). Belmont, CA: Wadsworth.

Kindig, D. (1975). Interdisciplinary education for primary health care team delivery. *Journal of Medical Education, 50*, 97-110.

Kleinman, A. (1980). *Patients and healers in the context of culture.* Berkeley: University of California Press.

Koester, J., Wiseman, R. L., & Sanders, J. A. (1993). Multiple perspectives on intercultural communication competence. In R. L. Wiseman & J. Koester (Eds.), *Intercultural communication competence* (pp. 3-15). Newbury Park, CA: Sage.

Kosa, J., & Zola, I. (Eds.). (1975). *Poverty and health: A sociological analysis.* Cambridge, MA: Harvard University Press.

Kotler, P., & Roberto, E. (1989). *Social marketing: Strategies for changing public behavior.* New York: Free Press.

Kreps, G. L. (1986). Health communication and the elderly. *World Communication, 15,* 55-70.

Kreps, G. L. (1987). Organizational sexism in health care. In L. Stewart & S. Ting-Toomey (Eds.), *Communication, gender and sex roles in diverse interaction contexts* (pp. 228-236). Norwood, NJ: Ablex.

Kreps, G. L. (1988a). Relational communication in health care. *Southern Communication Journal, 53,* 344-359.

Kreps, G. L. (1988b). The pervasive role of information in health and health care: Implications for health communication policy. In J. Anderson (Ed.), *Communication yearbook 11* (pp. 238-276). Newbury Park, CA: Sage.

Kreps, G. L. (1990a). *Organizational communication: Theory and practice* (2nd ed.). White Plains, NY: Longman.

Kreps, G. L. (1990b). A systematic analysis of health communication with the elderly. In H. Giles, N. Coupland, & J. Weimann (Eds.), *Communication, health, and the elderly* (pp. 135-154). Manchester, UK: Manchester University Press.

Kreps, G. L. (1990c). Communication and health education. In E. Berlin Ray & L Donohew (Eds.), *Communication and health: Systems and applications* (pp. 187-203). Hillsdale, NJ: Erlbaum.

Kreps, G. L. (1992). Multicultural relations in modern health care. *International Journal of Intercultural Relations, 16,* 316-324.

Kreps, G. L. (1993a). Promoting a sociocultural evolutionary approach to preventing sexual harassment: Metacommunication and cultural adaptation. In G. L. Kreps (Ed.), *Sexual harassment: Communication implications* (pp. 310-318). Cresskill, NJ: Hampton Press.

Kreps, G. L. (1993b, November). *Disability and culture: Effects on multicultural relations in modern organizations.* Paper presented to the Speech Communication Association conference, Miami, FL.

Kreps, G. L., & Query, J. L. (1989). The applications of communication competence: Assessment and testing in health care. In G. M. Phillips & J. T. Wood (Eds.), *Speech communication: Essays to commemorate the 75th anniversary of the Speech Communication Association* (pp. 293-323). Carbondale, IL: SIU Press.

Kreps, G. L., & Thornton, B. C. (1984). *Health communication: Theory and practice.* New York: Longman.

Kreps, G. L., & Thornton, B. C. (1992). *Health communication: Theory and Practice* (2nd ed.). Prospect Heights, IL: Waveland Press.

Kunimoto, E. N. (1977, May). *Multicultural communication and mental health.* Paper presented at the International Communication Association Conference, Berlin, West Germany.

Kunimoto, E. N. (1982). Communicating collegiality by satellite. *Pacific Islands Communication Journal, 2*(2), 137-143.

Lambert, W. (1991, November 19). Discrimination affects people with HIV. *Wall Street Journal,* pp. b1, b6.

Lambrinos, J. (1992). Tomorrow's workforce: Challenge for today. *The Bureaucrat, 20*(4), 27-29.

Lefebvre, C., & Flora, J. (1988). Social marketing and public health intervention. *Health Education Quarterly, 15,* 299-315.

Liu, W., & Duff, R. (1972). The strength of weak ties. *Public Opinion Quarterly, 36,* 361-366.

Locke, D. C. (Ed.). (1992). Increasing multicultural understanding. Newbury Park, CA: Sage.

Maibach, E. W. (1993). The use of behavioral theory in the development of AIDS information campaigns. In B. C. Thornton & G. L. Kreps (Eds.), *Perspectives on Health Communication* (pp. 207-217). Prospect Heights, IL: Waveland Press.

Maibach, E. W., Kreps, G. L., & Bonaguro, E. W. (1993). Developing strategic communication campaigns for HIV/AIDS prevention. In S. C. Ratzan (Ed.), *AIDS: Effective health communication for the 90s* (pp. 15-35). Washington, DC: Taylor & Francis.

Marshall, J. (1980). Stress amongst nurses. In C. L. Cooper & J. Marshall (Eds.), *White collar and professional stress* (pp. 19-59). New York: Wiley.

Martin, J. N. (1993). Intercultural communication competence: A review. In R. L. Wiseman & J. Koester (Eds.), *Intercultural communication competence* (pp. 16-29). Newbury Park, CA: Sage.

Martiney, R. (1978). *Hispanic culture and health care: Fact, fiction, and folklore.* St. Louis, MO: C. V. Mosby.

Masi, R. (1988). Multicultural medicine: Fad or forgotten concept? *Canadian Medical Association Journal, 140,* 1086-1087.

Maslach, C. (1982). *Burnout: The cost of caring.* Englewood Cliffs, NJ: Prentice Hall.

Maslow, A. H. (1943). A theory of human motivation. *Psychology Review, 50,* 370-396.

Maslow, A. H. (1954). *Motivation and personality.* New York: Harper & Row.

Mattson, S. (1989). Health care delivery to Southeast Asian refugees. *Migration World Magazine, 17*(1), 28-35.

McNeil, C. (1990). Culture: The impact on health care. *Journal of Cancer Education, 5*, 13-16.

Meisenheider, J. B., & LaCharite, C. L. (1989). Fear of contagion: A stress response in acquired immunodeficiency syndrome. *Advances in Nursing Science, 11*(2), 29-38.

Mendelsohn, R. S. (1979). *Confessions of a medical heretic.* Chicago: Contemporary Books.

Mendelsohn, R.S. (1981). *Male practice: How doctors manipulate women.* Chicago: Contemporary Books.

Mendelson, M. (1974). *Tender loving greed.* New York: Knopps.

Miller, K. I., Stiff, J. B., & Ellis, B. H. (1988). Communication and empathy as precursors to burnout among human service workers. *Communication Monographs, 55*, 250-265.

Mondragon, D., Kirkman-Liff, B., & Schneller, E. (1991). Hostility to people with AIDS: Risk perception and demographic factors. *Social Science and Medicine, 32*, 1137-1142.

Northouse, P. G., & Northouse, L. L. (1992). *Health communication: Strategies for health professionals* (2nd ed.). Norwalk, CT: Appleton & Lange.

O'Hair, D. (1986). Patient preferences for physician persuasion strategies. *Theoretical Medicine, 7*, 147-164.

O'Hair, D., O'Hair, M., Southward, M., & Krayer, K. (1987). Patient compliance and physician communication. *Journal of Compliance in Health Care, 2*, 125-128.

Osteria, T., & Sullivan, G. (1991). Importance of religious and cultural values in AIDS education programs in Malaysia and the Philippines. *AIDS Education and Prevention, 3*(2), 133-146.

Pegels, C. (1980). *Health care and the elderly.* Rockville, MD: Aspen.

Perrow, C. (1965). Hospitals, technology, structure and goals. In J. March (Ed.), *Handbook of organizations* (pp. 910-971). Chicago: Rand-McNally.

Peters, T. (1987). *Thriving on chaos.* New York: Knopf.

Peters-Golden, H. (1982). Breast cancer: Varied perceptions of social support in the illness experience. *Social Science and Medicine, 16*, 483- 491.

Portnoy, B., Anderson, D. M., & Eriksen, M. P. (1989). Application of diffusion theory to health promotion research. *Family and Community Health, 12*(3), 63-71.

Pratt, L., Seligmann, A., & Reader, G. (1957). Physicians' view on the level of medical information among patients. *American Journal of Public Health, 47*, 1277-1283.

Query, J. (1985, October). *Small group processes and support groups: An impetus.* Paper presented to the Speech Communication Association of Ohio, Columbus, OH.

Quesada, G., & Heller, R. (1977). Sociocultural barriers to medical care among Mexican-Americans in Texas. *Medical Care, 15*, 93-101.

Randall, T. (1991). Key to organ donation may be cultural awareness. *The Journal of the American Medical Association, 285*(2), 176-178.

Rapkin, A. J., & Erickson, P. I. (1990). Differences in knowledge of and risk factors for AIDS between Hispanic and non-Hispanic women attending an urban family planning clinic. *AIDS, 4*(9), 889-899.

Ray, E. B. (1987). Support relationships and occupational stress in the workplace. In T. L. Albrecht & M. B. Adelman (Eds.), *Communicating social support* (pp. 172-191). Newbury Park, CA: Sage.

Ray, E. B., & Miller, K. I. (1990). Communication in health care organizations. In E. B. Ray & L. Donohew (Eds.), *Communication and health* (pp. 92-107). Hillsdale, NJ: Lawrence Erlbaum.

Ribble, D. (1989). Psychosocial support groups for people with HIV infection and AIDS. *Holistic Nursing Practice, 3*, 52-62.

Richman, J. M. (1989). Social support for hospice workers. *Home Healthcare Nurse, 7*, 8-38.

Rogers, E. M. (1983) *Diffusion of innovations.* New York: Free Press.

Rogers, E. M., & Argarwal-Rogers, R. (1976). *Communication in organizations.* New York: Free Press.

Ross, J. W., Bayley, C., Michel, V., & Pugh, D. (1986). *Handbook for hospital ethics committees.* Chicago: American Hospital Association.

Rossiter, C. M., & Pearce, W. B. (1975). *Communicating personally: A theory of interpersonal communication and human relationships.* Indianapolis: Bobbs-Merrill.

Roter, D. (1983). Physician/patient communication: Transmission of information and patient effects. *Maryland State Medical Journal, 32*, 260- 265.

Schlesinger, A. M. (1992). *The disuniting of America: Reflections on a multicultural society.* New York: Norton.

Schutz, W. (1958). *A three-dimensional theory of interpersonal behavior.* New York: Holt, Rinehart, & Winston.

Seligmann, A., McGrath, N., & Pratt, L. (1957). Level of medication information among clinic patients. *Journal of Chronic Disorders, 6*, 497- 509.

Shilts, R. (1987). *And the band played on: Politics, people, and the AIDS epidemic.* New York: St. Martin's.

Siegal, B. S. (1986). *Love, medicine, and miracles.* New York: Harper & Row.

Sodowsky, G. R., & Taffe, R. C. (1991). Counselor trainees' analyses of multicultural counseling videotapes. *Journal of Multicultural Counseling and Development, 19*(3), 115-129.

Spector, R. E. (1979). *Cultural diversity in health and illness.* New York: Appleton-Century-Crofts.

Starr, P. (1982). *The social transformation of American medicine.* New York: Basic Books.

Strauss, A., Fagerhaugh, W., Suczek, & Weiner, C. (1991, July/August). AIDS and health care deficiencies. *Society*, pp. 63-73.

Sykora, R. (1991). *The mass media: Its ability to influence public opinion.* Unpublished thesis. Department of Communication, University of Hawaii.

Takahashi, Y. (1990). Informing a patient of malignant illness: Commentary from a cross-cultural viewpoint. *Death Studies, 14*(1), 83-91.

Thornton, B. C. (1978). Health care teams and multi-methodological research. In B. Ruben (Ed.), *Communication yearbook 2* (pp. 538-553). New Brunswick, NJ: Transaction Press.

Thornton, B. C. (1993). The ethics committee as a small group. In B. C. Thornton & G. L. Kreps (Eds.), *Perspectives on health communication* (pp. 92-97). Prospect Heights, IL: Waveland Press.

Thornton, B. C., McCoy, E., & Baldwin, D. (1980). Interdisciplinary health care teams. In D. Baldwin, B. Rowley, & V. Williams (Eds.), *Interdisciplinary health care teams in teaching and practice.* Reno, NV: New Health Perspectives.

Tones, B. K. (1986). Health education and the ideology of health promotion: A review of alternative approaches. *Health Education Research, 1,* 3-12.

Treichler, P. A. (1987). AIDS, homophobia, and biomedical discourse: An epidemic of signification. *Cultural Studies, 1*(3), 263-305.

Treichler, P. A. (1988). AIDS, gender, and biomedical discourse: Current contests for meaning. In E. Fee & D. M. Fox (Eds.), *AIDS: The burdens of history* (pp. 190-266). Berkeley, CA: University of California Press.

Trice, H., & Beyer, J. (1984). Studying organizational cultures through rites and ceremonials. *Academy of Management Review, 28,* 653- 659.

UCLA Bulletin. (1992). Alexander's Grad. Class Notes. *UCLA Magazine, 3*(2), 72.

U.S. Senate Special Committee on Aging, Subcommittee on Long Term Care. (1974). *Nursing home care in the United States, failure in public policy: Introductory report.* Washington, DC: Government Printing Office.

U.S. Senate Special Committee on Aging, Subcommittee on Long Term Care. (1975). *Nursing home care in the United States, failure in public policy: Introductory report and nine supporting papers.* Washington, DC: Government Printing Office.

Waitzkin, H., & Stoekle, J. (1972). The communication of information about illness. *Advances in Psychosomatic Medicine, 8,* 180-215.

Waitzkin, H., & Stoekle, J. (1976). Information and control in the micropolitics of health care: Summary of an ongoing research project. *Social Science and Medicine, 10,* 236-276.

Watzlawick, P., Beavin, J., & Jackson, D. (1967). *Pragmatics of human communication.* New York: Norton.

Waxler-Morrison, N., Anderson, J., & Richardson, E. (Eds.). (1990). *Cross-cultural caring: A handbook for health professionals in Western Canada.* Vancouver, British Columbia: UBC Press.

Weick, K. (1979). *The social psychology of organizing* (2nd ed.). Reading, MA: Addison-Wesley.

Weiss, S. M. (1985). The federal role in disease prevention and health promotion. *American Psychologist, 40*(2), 234-235.

White, E. (1974). Health and the black person: An annotated bibliography. *American Journal of Nursing, 74,* 1839-1841.

Williams, C. L., & Berry, J. W. (1991). Primary prevention of acculturative stress among refugees: Application of psychological theory and practice. *American Psychologist, 48*(6), 632-641.

Wise, H. (1974). *Making health teams work.* Cambridge, MA: Ballinger.

Wohl, J. (1989). Integration of cultural awareness into psychotherapy. *American Journal of Psychotherapy, 11*(3), 343-356.

Wood, J. B. (1989). Communicating with older adults in health care settings: Cultural and ethnic considerations. Special issue: Developing leadership in geriatric education. *Educational Gerontology, 15*(4), 351- 362.

Wyatt, N. (1991) Physician-patient relationships: What do doctors say? *Health Communication, 3*, 157-174.

Yanda, R. (1977). *Doctors as managers of health care teams*. New York: AMACOM.

Author Index

Subject Index

About the Authors

Gary L. Kreps is Professor of Communication Studies and a Faculty Member of both the Gerontology and the International Training and Consultation programs at Northern Illinois University. His B.A. and M.A. degrees are from the University of Colorado and his Ph.D. degree is from the University of Southern California. He has held faculty positions at Purdue, Indiana, and Rutgers Universities and served as a senior research fellow with the National Cancer Institute framing national policy for cancer information dissemination. His many books and articles examine the role of communication in health care and organizational life, and he recently edited a special issue of the *American Behavioral Scientist* titled "Communicating to Promote Health."

Elizabeth N. Kunimoto is Associate Professor and Undergraduate Chair in the Department of Communication at the University of Hawaii-Manoa in Honolulu, Hawaii. She earned a B.A. in Speech Pathology at the University of Michigan, and an M.A. in Speech and a Ph.D. in Educational Psychology at the University of Hawaii. Besides teaching and advising students comprising a rainbow of diversity in cultures, she finds that as a certified psychologist her courses in communication provide an ideal context for the prevention of psychopathology and the enhancement of personal health. Using a modification of the Primary Prevention Model, she presents multicultural communication proficiency as a major tool in reducing the stress factors that lead to psychopathology. She believes that through proficiency in multicultural communication a person can gain knowledge, gain skills, and develop attitudes that would enhance personal health. She finds that Hawaii's multi-ethnic population offers a wealth of approaches to health care and that communication is the leading edge that harmonizes East-West perspectives.